*

BEYOND·RACE

A NEW VISION OF COMMUNITY IN AMERICA

*

BEYOND·RACE

A NEW VISION OF COMMUNITY IN AMERICA

Ogom P. Nwosu

TSEHAI
Publishers & Distributors

UNISA
university of south africa
PRESS

LOS ANGELES | PRETORIA | NEW YORK | ADDIS ABABA

TSEHAI
Publishers & Distributors

UNISA
university
of south africa
PRESS

Beyond Race: A New Vision of Community in America
Copyright © 2009 by Ogom P. Nwosu. All rights reserved.

Tsehai books may be purchased for educational, business, or sales promotional use. For more information, please contact our special sales department.

First Edition: 2009

Tsehai Publishers and Distributors
Loyola Marymount University
1 LMU Drive, UH 3012, Los Angeles, CA 90045

ISBN: 978-1-59907-038-4

www.tsehaipublishers.com

UNISA Press
P O Box 392, Unisa, Muckleneuk, 0003
South Africa

ISBN: 978-1-86888-546-6

www.unisa.ac.za/press

Publisher: Elias Wondimu | Editor: Mary S. Lederer
Cover Photography and Design: Endrias Zewde [www.endriasdesign.com]
Typesetting: Yoseph Gezahegne | Editorial Assistant: James Mollison

Library of Congress Catalog Card Number
A catalog record for this book is available from the Library of Congress.

British Library Cataloguing in Publication Data
A catalogue record for this book is available from the British Library.

10 9 8 7 6 5 4 3 2 1

Printed in the United States of America

To the memory of my dearest sister

Mary Chinelo Nwosu

Contents

Acknowledgments

It has taken more than four years to complete this work. The vicissitudes of life—the deaths of my only sister Mary and of my mother Cecilia, two giants in my life—and other scholarly and administrative commitments both locally and internationally have meant changes in completion date. But these realities of life have given added meaning to the book. My mother, who passed away in 2005 after a prolonged battle with diabetes, encouraged the completion of this book, and believing in the impermanence of life, she spoke always of the need to do good, "for no one knows tomorrow," a statement that draws strength from the age-old African proverb, "No condition is permanent." My life's work has been an unflinching and inviolate commitment to this vision of justice today and tomorrow.

This commitment is also reflected in the current work. The voices that have helped to refine it have been diverse. I am enormously grateful to my graduate assistant, Alejandro Barrios, who, like me, believes that the fundamental crisis in American society today is the national obsession with race, complicated by deep-seated notions about how to treat each other fairly. Both of us poured through hundreds of research documents in the course of preparing this book. One person who also deserves mention is Al Neighorn, my former graduate student, now in the School of Dance, Theater, and Arts Administration at the University of Akron at Akron, Ohio. Al reviewed all chapters, made useful suggestions for modifications, and engaged in several hours of telephone conversations with me about the book. To Dr. Samuel Brown, Senior Fellow at the Schaefer Center for Public Policy, University of Baltimore, I say thank you for taking the time to review the book and for offering suggestions. Sam and I graduated from Towson State University, Towson, Maryland, many years ago; we have kept in contact, and frequently have engaged in discussions regarding race and public policy in America. These discussions have also inspired this book. I am equally grateful to my good friend Myron Lustig of San Diego State University, a past president of the Western States Communication Association, who read the draft, saw tremendous value in the book's ability to improve human relations among the various sectors of our society, and urged quick completion. I extend my deepest appreciation to Professors Virginia Kidd, John Hwang, and Lawrence Chase at California State University, Sacramento and Professor Gozie Ogbodo of Golden Gate University, San Francisco, for their thoughtful reviews and suggestions for strengthening the initial drafts.

My graduate students (a very diverse class) at California State University, Sacramento, where I taught for many years, reviewed several chapters of the book and offered their critiques. The feedback that emerged from classroom discussions in my graduate seminar on contemporary issues in intercultural communication has helped to clarify the arguments and the need for this book. I am very grateful to them. I am equally grateful to Professor Don Taylor, a dear friend and colleague, and Director of Academic Planning and Quality in the Office of Academic Affairs at California State University, Sacramento, for his insights. I thank the publisher Allyn and Bacon, for their permission to incorporate in this book a revised version of my work on cultural adjustment, which drew from my experiences living in the United States, and had originally appeared in their book: AmongUs written by Myron Lustig and Jolene Koester. To Elias Wondimu and Tsehai Publishers at Loyola Marymount University, Los Angeles, California, who believed in the value of this work for improving our relations with each other and the rest of the world, I say thank you. Elias and I met in 2007 in Beverly Hills at an event hosted by Don Cheadle and John Prendergast to end the Genocide in Darfur and beyond. Thereafter we met on countless occasions over tea and dinner to discuss the challenges of race and ethnic relations, a subject that he has also devoted his life's work to. It was Elias who prodded the completion of this book, believing that its content had tremendous value for forging a new community among peoples of varying racial and ethnic backgrounds. I also want to express my enormous gratitude to my editor, Mary S. Lederer. She was patient with me as we went through several iterations of the manuscript, and she offered sound editorial suggestions that further strengthened the book. I cannot end without acknowledging our Creator, the giver of all knowledge, without whose guidance this book would not have been a reality. Finally, the errors and omissions in this book are mine, and I take full responsibility.

1

BEYOND RACE: A NEW DIALOGUE OF ENGAGEMENT

A candid examination of race matters takes us to the core of the crisis of American democracy. And the degree to which race matters in the plight and predicament of fellow citizens is a crucial measure of whether we can keep alive the best of this democratic experiment we call America.

Cornel West

Race is for me a more onerous burden than AIDS. My disease is the result of biological factors over which we … have had no control. Racism … is entirely made by people, and therefore it hurts … infinitely more.

Arthur Ashe

I think America is at the point now where if a white person has the time to get to know who you are, that they are willing on average to look beyond race and judge you as an individual. That doesn't mean that they've stopped making snap judgments. It doesn't mean that … if I got into an elevator, a woman might not clutch her purse a little tighter. Or if I'm walking down the street, that you might not hear some clicks of doors locking, right. I mean, there's still a host of stereotypes that I think a lot of people are operating under. But I think if they have time to get to know you, they will judge you as they would judge anybody else, and I think that's enormous progress. We've made progress. Yes, things are better. But better is not good enough. And we've still got a long way to go.

Barack Obama

There's no law you can pass to eliminate hatred if it's in people's hearts, but you can make harmony a national goal.

James Carville

Beyond Race

On October 3, 1995, the jury hearing the case of football great O. J. Simpson in the murder trial of his ex-wife Nicole Brown Simpson and her friend Ronald Goldman rendered its verdict. "In the matter of the people of the State of California versus Orenthal James Simpson, case number BA097211, we the jury in the above entitled action find the defendant, Orenthal James Simpson, not guilty of the crime of murder...."[1] It was a verdict that shocked mostly white America. The criminal trial had been lengthy, lasting nearly nine months, involving 120 witnesses, 45,000 pages of evidence, and 1,100 exhibits.

At the time the verdict was announced, I was a faculty member at California State University, Sacramento. The indescribable silence across this predominantly white institution of higher education was unbelievable. One could almost hear a pin drop on this pristine campus. It was a day of quiet mourning and outrage. In many offices across the country, the reaction was similar. White America was stunned that a man they strongly believed had murdered his ex-wife and her friend in cold blood was let go by the justice system.

But America is a nation of laws, and once the justice system renders a decision, life must go on, no matter how distasteful to us the decision might be. President Clinton, who had watched the verdict from the Oval Office, issued a statement: "The jury heard the evidence and rendered its verdict. Our system of justice requires respect for their decision. At this moment our thoughts and prayers should be with the families of the victims of this terrible crime."[2]

In black America, there was a sense of relief—relief born out of deep indignation and lingering grievances against a justice system that America's most vocal minority has long perceived as patently lacking in fairness and integrity. In this instance, one of their own was only lucky to go free—only lucky. But there was also a sense of anguish in black America. It was anguish growing out of an assessment of how socio-economic conditions might have influenced the verdict's outcome. The reasoning in black America was that the verdict would have been different had O. J. Simpson been poor. This reasoning drew on a sorry picture of countless numbers of African Americans who have been executed or were and still are sitting in jailhouses across America, many of them innocent, but because they are poor and black, they have been unable to obtain the kind of legal representation that would set them free. With his fame and wealth, however, the football star was able to assemble some of the best legal minds in the country. Together, these lawyers mounted a vigorous and successful defense in his name.

The Simpson verdict of not guilty loomed large in my mind that morning of October 3 as I pondered its impact on race relations in America, and how to directly engage this complicated subject in a conversation with my students. One of the courses that I taught focused on the challenges and promises of communication in a multicultural and multiracial society. There was a certain expectation that the verdict would have a place in class discussions. But the problem of how to broach this emotive topic in a mixed class of white, black, brown, and red students, already discomforted by the verdict, weighed heavily on my mind.

Indeed, a white colleague who had come to value my expertise on issues of race and diversity asked me moments after the verdict what I thought, as we met in the hallways of the department. "I really don't know," I responded honestly. "I know he killed her. It had to be," she whispered quickly in a hushed tone. One could sense her agitation. My colleague believed that my expertise on the subject of race relations, and perhaps more importantly my background as a foreign-born United States citizen of African descent, offered me the capacity to provide a more neutral and objective assessment of race-related events in the U. S. As an African-born black, I was trusted. She seemed comfortable. I have always wondered whether my friend and colleague would have brought up such a racially-charged subject had I been an American-born black.

I have come to understand, from a historical perspective, that Americans, especially white and black, have almost always demonstrated a certain discomfort when talking with each other about race. Indeed, my experience suggests that on matters of race, most white or black Americans would rather engage in conversation with new immigrants. It is a comfort zone in which the conversation does not appear to assign blame. But most blacks and other minorities expect that the new immigrant will stand with them.

Naturally, I pondered my colleague's emphatic remarks about who killed Nicole Simpson and Ron Goldman; I paused for a moment, and then responded with a quiet tone. "We really don't know if O. J. killed Nicole or Mr. Goldman." I chose my words carefully, with empathy and a deep sense of anguish. I did not want to worsen the pain and the anger that most of white America felt as a result of the verdict. I added as a point of fact, "You know, it would be difficult for anyone to claim that he or she knows, since none of us witnessed the murders." I was not a lawyer, and I was not about to play one. I did not sit on the jury, but I know it must have been a difficult task. And, and given my faith, since I was not God, I was not prepared to render judgment.

I was aware from the various news reports that not a single person witnessed the brutal stabbing death of both Nicole Brown Simpson and Ronald Goldman. I was also aware that the evidence presented by the prosecution was only circumstantial and highly controvertible. Any conviction in a murder trial, not the least this one, would require evidence beyond reasonable doubt. That is the law. My response to my colleague produced some consternation in her countenance. She looked at me directly in the face for a few seconds. Perhaps in shock, she thundered, "How could you say such things?" in understandable anger. Then silence followed, and a very awkward feeling consumed me. Quick seconds later, we both gingerly left the scene to run our separate errands. Not a word of good-bye or "I will see you later" was uttered.

For several days, that very conversation left a sour taste in my mouth. Was I insensitive? Was I too direct? Or was I brutally frank and honest? Or was I expected to take sides in the complicated black-white discourse on race in America? As noted earlier, too often new immigrants, and indeed many newcomers to America, depending on the color of their skin or ethnic ancestry, are called upon to take a stand on the emotive issue of race in America. And gradually, whether they like it or not, they become mired in the grand debate. And yes, as new entrants to America, new immigrants must participate in that dialogue. Their lives, their experiences, and their interactions will be shaped by it, as it has shaped the lives, experiences, and interactions of whites, blacks, Native American Indians, and other American racial groups.

The simple fact is that race continues to matter in this country. In every aspect of public or social life in America, race counts: in the bedrooms and in the boardrooms; in nearly every public discussion and decision; in the construction and implementation of public policies and programs; in employment and hiring practices; in contracting services; in housing and public accommodation; in infrastructure development, including where to site a penal institution or build low-cost housing for low income earners, or construct a clinic; in the educational system, including admission practices at colleges and universities; in public policies about health, including policies on children, on foster care and adoption, on HIV/AIDS, and on the environment; in jury selection and in decision-making in the courts; and in the arena of entertainment and sports. The list goes on. The simple truth is that discussions and decisions about nearly every facet of American life are shaped by race. And many times, the polemic and the outcomes leave us more frustrated, more suffocated, and more polarized. Having lived in the U. S. for nearly two decades, I have become unquestionably convinced that the American project of the twenty-first century must be to find ways to propel America beyond race. It is to this task that I have devoted this book: to prod and to challenge all Americans on the need for a meaningful, constructive, and honest dialogue on race. The absence of such a dialogue reflects a continuing crisis of meaning on matters of race in our country, and the challenges posed by it on our democratic experiment.

Clearly, the deaths of Nicole Brown Simpson and Ronald Goldman were tragic. But the evidence against Simpson in the high-class, high-drama case, presided over by Judge Lance A. Ito of the Superior Court of the State of California, was foggy. Simpson's defense team, led by the famed attorney Johnnie Cochran, was able to sow sufficient doubt in the minds of the jury. "If the glove don't fit, you must acquit" became Cochran's clarion call. In truth, the glove found by white Los Angeles police detective Mark Fuhrman on the scene of the murder did not fit Simpson's hands. In black America, there was already a general perception that Simpson was framed. Fuhrman's shaky testimony further escalated that perception.

Under oath, Fuhrman, a police officer with several years of experience, told the jury that he had never used racial slurs or ethnophaulisms against African Americans. But as evidence would later show, in taped police ride-along conversations, the officer had repeatedly used the pejorative word *nigger* in his line of duty. More than ten years since the case ended, we still do not know the motive for providing such testimony. And to this day, we still do not know who murdered Nicole Simpson and Ron Goldman. But whatever the reason, Fuhrman's false testimony on whether he had used racial slurs in his line of duty clouded any possibility of truth and credibility regarding his entire evidence before the court.

Before the Simpson case, there were reports and investigations of evidence tampering, evidence planting, and evidence distortion in the Los Angeles Police Department—reports that had shaken public confidence, in particular in the minority community, in law enforcement. Thus, in the wake of these reports, Fuhrman's testimony ultimately may have dealt a serious blow to the prosecution's case. Immediately race, as had been predicted, became one of the most significant signature tunes in the defense's argument to free Simpson. After less than four hours of deliberations, the ten-woman, two-man jury, comprised of nine blacks, two whites, and one Hispanic, had no choice but to acquit. In the absence of evidence beyond reasonable doubt, the jury set the former football player free. It was a monumental setback for the prosecution and for the Los Angeles District Attorney's office, led at the time by Gil Garcetti.

During the trial, Garcetti met with prominent leaders of the black community in Los Angeles to assure them that his office would not seek the death penalty against Simpson. Garcetti recognized the historic distrust in black America of law enforcement and the justice system. Thus his pledge to African American leaders that the prosecution would not seek the death penalty against Simpson was designed to alleviate the distrust. By making that pledge, Garcetti was convinced that jurors of minority background serving in the Simpson trial might be more willing to render a guilty verdict—one that would consign Simpson to jail for the rest of his life. At the center of Garcetti's strategy was the prospect of jury nullification. His goal was to minimize any possibility that race might be introduced in the case. However, as we saw, race quickly became a factor.

I agree with Randall Kennedy of Harvard University Law School that "The decision to deprive a person of liberty pursuant to trial on criminal misconduct requires a remarkably high level of consensus." I also agree with Kennedy that "no other setting in America's political culture opens the door so widely to minorities for the exercise of power" as the jury process. "One dissenter on a jury is all that is required to prevent a conviction."[3] Garcetti's strategy was to prevent a dissenter, one dissenting black juror, but there was none in the Simpson case. The decision of the jury to acquit Simpson was not a consensus. The decision was unanimous, precisely because the evidence presented by the prosecution was seriously contaminated and thus controvertible, leaving no room for a verdict to convict.

In retrospect, the crux of the Simpson trial was not whether O. J. was innocent or guilty. The crux of the trial became race and the discourse regarding it. The dichotomy of perceptions and opinions on the case in both white and black America reflected the stubborn persistence of a long but troubling pattern in America's racial dilemma. In the eyes of black America, Simpson was framed. In the eyes of white America, Simpson was guilty. Public opinion polls after the verdict was announced showed an overwhelming majority of whites believing that Simpson had committed the murders, with a similar majority of blacks insisting that the football great was framed. Nothing in the mass media before or after the trial elevated the discourse on race relations. Talk show hosts and talking heads, including the so-called pundits and analysts, took sides on the matter depending on their racial background. Nothing in their conversations helped the discourse. The situation, sadly, has not changed as I write. How does one begin to craft a vision of genuine community in an environment of strong racial distrust?

Back in June 1998, a black man, James Byrd, Jr., was chained to a pick-up truck and dragged to his death by three white men: John King, Lawrence Brewer, and Shawn Berry. The three men had gone out for a drive on that fateful day. After some drinking, they went crazy—forcefully picked up Byrd, who lived in the same city, chained him to the back of their truck, and then dragged him for three miles until his body disintegrated.

The horrible incident, which took place in the small town of Jasper, Texas, shocked the nation. After the three men were convicted, PBS commissioned two film crews, one black and one white, to document the aftermath of the murders and to see what lessons could be drawn for improving race relations. The result was a documentary entitled Two Towns of Jasper, which became the cornerstone for a town-hall meeting of Jasper citizens hosted by Ted Koppel of ABC's Nightline.

The documentary, produced by two friends—Whitney Dow who is white and Marco Williams who is black—revealed a troubling reality behind the public demonstration of racial unity and outrage from the city's leaders. Beneath the public demonstration was a history of mutual distrust between blacks and whites in the town, and widely differing views about the state of race relations in the region. Indeed some white Jasper citizens expressed anger at the negative attention the incident had brought to their town. Other white citizens of Jasper were surprised that the incident took place in their town, and they tried to minimize the nature of the crime by blaming the personal failings of James Byrd as responsible for his tragedy. For black citizens of Jasper, the brutal murder of James Byrd was just more evidence of the prevailing racial attitudes and tension, as well as more evidence of hate in both the town and the region.

Whitney Dow commented after the documentary that Two Towns of Jasper is not so much about the murder of James Byrd, Jr. as it is about two perspectives on the murder. "The facts, after all, weren't in doubt," notes Dow. "It's a question of how you explain those facts. Listening to the black and white communities of Jasper talk about the crime turned out to be a pretty startling revelation of the depth of the division that exists between black and white Americans.[4]"

Marco Williams commented as follows: "Whitney and I spent a lot of time talking about the Byrd murder and how a film might excavate its deeper meaning. We were both horrified, of course … But the more we talked the more we experienced moments where our viewpoints diverged. We realized the divergences were rooted in our racial identities, our different racial experiences."[5]

In fact, the ninety-minute town hall meeting hosted by Ted Koppel to discuss the state of race relations in the town did little to change the strongly divergent views from both communities on the complex issue of race. A disappointed Ted Koppel summed up his view of that meeting this way: "If ever the differing perceptions of an event by members of the black and white communities in one town underscored the continuing racial divide that exists in this country, it is the murder of James Byrd, Jr. in Jasper, Texas."[6]

The most recent survey conducted by the Pew Center and National Public Radio in 2007 show no dramatic shift in black-white perceptions on racial discrimination in America. Among African Americans, 67 percent believe that blacks experience discrimination in employment; 65 percent say the same discrimination occurs in housing; 50 percent claim discrimination occurs when eating at restaurants or when shopping; and 43 percent claim the same bias occurs in college admission processes. By a margin of two to one, or larger, whites believe that "blacks rarely face bias" in any of these situations.[7]

A survey conducted in July 2007 of 600 metropolitan Detroit residents also shows a huge chasm between black and white America on matters of race.[8] White America believes blacks have an equal chance to get jobs for which they are qualified, housing they can afford, and fair treatment in the criminal justice system. Blacks disagree. While racial attitudes continue to soften, the results of these surveys reflect long-held perceptions that are barriers to overcoming the troubling pattern of divisions in America's racial history.

Perhaps it is important to ask why these divisions about race relations persist. And how do we move beyond them? For American blacks, the perception is grounded in historical inequities, which continue to affect the realities of everyday existence in the U. S. For white America, the perception about race relations derives from a belief that a "color-blind" society is now preferable, despite historical inequities. Speaking about the experiences of both groups, Michigan State University professor of urban geography Joe Darden notes, "There is a higher likelihood that blacks would have experienced housing discrimination. The assumption of whites is that if they haven't experienced it, it must not happen. They may believe this is the U. S. and everyone is free and discrimination has ended."[9] Differing perceptions about anything are a part of the human experience. How those human experiences manifest themselves in processes of human interaction and create patterns of inequities is invariably the basis for racial tension. Bridging the black-white perceptions about race must be central in any dialogue designed to move our nation beyond race. Understanding these perceptions is the first step in this process.

The first view—the black position—wants an acknowledgement of the historical inequities and feels a fierce urgency to factor this position into the crafting and implementation of public policies and programs in America. The second view—the white position—reluctantly acknowledges the historical inequities, argues that the inequities are fading, that disparities in current status are a matter of individual effort by themselves or families, not a racial issue, and calls on Americans to get over it. In this context, to factor historical wrongs into the development and implementation of public policies and programs would amount to replacing one form of discrimination with another.

James Carville, political strategist for the Democrats, summed it this way: "Too many white people say, 'Look, we've had these programs and we've done our part and that's it, to hell with them.' And too many black people say, 'We've been victims of racism and we continue to be victims of racism, to hell with them.' It's a very difficult place for our country to be—one where there doesn't seem to be too much room for brotherhood and common ground."[10]

Thus the discourse on race relations has become a struggle between those who historically have been denied opportunity and privilege strictly on the basis of the color of their skin, and those who have been given opportunity and privilege strictly on the basis of the color of their skin. It has been a discourse on what is just and what is fair. It really is a hard place for a country to be in, but it is not insurmountable. A new vision of community in America requires a genuine conversation on race—a new dialogue of engagement.

Differing black-white perceptions on race remain a persistent fixture of public conversations in America. Every now and then, we are reminded about it—either in terms of small acts of meanness that go unreported or in terms of large acts of meanness that we are fortunate to witness on television (and that consequently provide additional ammunition for those who believe that more work is needed to move our nation beyond race). It was present in Jena, Louisiana in 2007, during the Jena Six incident involving a group of six black teenagers charged with the beating of Justin Barker, a white teenager. It was present in 2003 in the ABC/PBS town-hall meeting in Jasper, Texas. It was present in the courtroom discourse, in both the criminal and civil trials, about Simpson's guilt or innocence in the 1990s. True, the O. J. Simpson case gave the mass media its biggest news stories of the 1990s: it generated ninety magazine covers, not including countless newspaper headlines and analyses; it gave talk radio its highest-ever ratings—a twelve-plus share in Arbitron ratings—and it helped launch a new cable network, Court TV.[11]

The public conversations unfortunately also led to differing and troubling outcomes. In fact, the subsequent trial of Simpson in a civil proceeding produced a bizarre outcome—what Jeffrey Abramson of Brandeis University calls "two juries, two societies, two codes of justice."[12] In the civil trial, the jury of nine whites, one Hispanic, one Asian, and one person of black and Hispanic ancestry, found Simpson guilty of murder, and slapped him with a hefty fine of $8.5 million. John Mack, president of the Los Angeles Urban League, an African American civil rights organization, said of the guilty verdict in the civil trial, "It was payback time for white America."[13] Such remarks from a prominent African American leader paint a stark portrait of the depth, breadth, and emotional sentiment surrounding America's racial gulf. Another event occurs, and each side waits for its time and turn to pay back. How do we break this cycle?

The O. J. Simpson case; the Rodney King incident; the beating of Reginald Denny, a white truck driver in South Central Los Angeles, by black youth following the King verdict; the dragging death of James Byrd, Jr. in Texas by three white men; the death of Amadou Diallo, the West African immigrant from Guinea who was reportedly shot forty-one times by then-Mayor Giuliani's Street Crime Unit in New York; the violence in Cincinnati involving the shooting death of nineteen-year old Timothy Thomas, a black youth, by a white police officer; the case of fourteen-year-old Donovan, an African American teenager from Los Angeles, captured on video as he was being punched on the face and slammed on the hood of a police car by a white police officer after he had been subdued; and a long list of racially motivated discord in America remind us that, as a nation, we remain disconnected, lacking in understanding of each other.

The simple truth is that we remain a nation of strangers, continually fixated on race. Whites hang on to it, consciously and unconsciously, because it has always benefited them. Blacks want to hang on to it consciously—because it might benefit them. The quest for a society in which each person is judged by the content of his or her character has become, sadly, just a quest. Given the current state of race relations, it seems that we have made nonsense of the true meaning of the Latin phrase engraved in our currency, E pluribus unum: from many, we form one. Today, E pluribus unum remain mere words, meaningless, to say the least, in our psyche, and in our relations with each other.

How do we build a more perfect union when we continuously view one another with fear and suspicion; when we repeatedly assess any move made by others through distorted lenses; when we attribute wrong motives because it plays in our favor; when we perpetuate long-standing cultural and racial stereotypes, and make decisions and construct national policies based on them—decisions on whether one gets a job or not, on whether one gets accommodation or not, and on whether one gets pulled over by the police or not. Fairness and equity continue to be defined in ways that suit us. These actions, like it or not, lead us in the direction of a more imperfect union. We have forgotten that the formation of one from many, E pluribus unum, is a work in progress, requiring genuine dialogue and engagement, requiring understanding, and a genuine sense of fairness.

As we have seen throughout our nation's history, the formation of one from many is simply not enough. How the many get along—work together, live together, build together, share together, suffer together, and enjoy together—must be a central concern of our national discourse. The task of fashioning a genuine American community emerges from this process. We cannot build this community without an understanding of each other. The American project of the twenty-first century must focus on a new dialogue of engagement. I agree with Cornel West that how we set up the terms for discussing the racial issues will shape our perception of one another and our response to these issues. But I disagree with West that only race matters. I am clearly convinced that continuing the fixation, in a polarizing manner, on race in our national dialogue offers limited hope for racial understanding, racial reconciliation, or racial consensus.

We cannot think or look beyond race, however, if we remain in denial of the challenges posed by race, or if we continue to refuse to deal directly and head-on with issues posed by it. Nothing in our recent past suggests that race is something that can easily be wished away just by snapping our fingers. The remarks from Chicago Tribune columnist Clarence Page are instructive here: "Many demand that we 'get past race.' But denials of a cancer, no matter how vigorous they may be, will not make the malignancy go away."[14]

So what must we do? It seems to me that a new dialogue of engagement, requiring us to deal directly with race, represents an essential framework for looking beyond race. This is the focus of this book. The differing perceptions and realities regarding long-standing historic and institutional inequities and inequalities in America cannot be changed unless we reverse, and quickly too, the terms and the parameters for discussing racial issues in our nation. The dichotomy between blacks and whites, for example, on any issue of significance in our country ought to remind us of the urgent need for genuine dialogue among Americans—in ways that catapult our nation beyond race.

Our diversity remains the single most important communication challenge of the twenty-first century. If we do not manage the diversity now, the diversity will manage us. In other words, if we do not develop a systematic approach to managing our differences, then our differences will become impossible to manage over time. Now is the time to seize the challenge. At the present time, there is no serious dialogue on the issue.

2

RACE AND THE QUESTION OF FAIRNESS

Fairness is a complex and contextual organizational and communication concept and process requiring the application of different norms in decision-making and resource allocation.

Ogom P. Nwosu

When race-based action is necessary to further a compelling governmental interest, such action does not violate the constitutional guarantee of equal protection so long as the narrow-tailoring requirement is also satisfied. Context matters when reviewing race-based governmental action under the Equal Protection Clause.

Sandra Day O'Connor

[T]he only time we scream "Unfair!" as a nation is when the beneficiaries are people of color.

Troy Duster

A vigorous enforcement of civil rights will bring an end to segregated public facilities, but it cannot bring an end to fears, prejudice, pride and irrationality, which are the barriers to a truly integrated society.

Martin Luther King, Jr.

Race and the Question of Fairness

An examination of the conversation on race in America shows that it is a conversation fundamentally linked to the question of fairness. This conversation, however, assumes a universal application of the norm of fairness, ignoring the complexity of its application as embodied in our democratic experiment. Scholars such as John Rawls, Robert Nozick, and Jennifer Hochschild, among others, have written extensively on notions of fairness, and their works provide some theoretical underpinnings of the concept in the context of political, social, and economic inequalities.[15]

An analysis of the discussions in the literature suggests the concept of fairness, like democracy, is very complicated. It is complicated because it is an emotive notion and means different things to different people. Hence we find in different contexts different interpretations and manifestations of the concept. Like democracy, fairness is also time-consuming, yet it is indispensable to the stability of a civil society. It is absolutely the one thing we must do right to avoid chaos and lawlessness in a society that is increasingly diverse. It is precisely for these reasons that a genuine conversation on fairness is absolutely essential to moving our nation beyond race.

Historical Context

One of the most venerated principles of fairness embodied in our democratic experiment is equality under the law. The Fourteenth Amendment to the U. S. Constitution that deals with the Equal Protection Clause requires that states and their functioning agents apply the law equally and not give preference to one person or class of persons over another. This requirement means that states are only obligated, at most, to treat people the same if they are similarly situated or "similarly circumstanced." They are not obligated, however, to treat all persons or groups in the same manner.

Based on the above principle of fairness, states enact legislation involving classifications that either advantage or disadvantage one group of persons. For example, the permissible age for alcohol consumption is twenty-one years in several states and eighteen in others. Accordingly, those under this age are not allowed to purchase alcohol. The differential treatment is based on age, and most people have not questioned the fairness of the legislation that informed this classification. However, when the disparate treatment is based on race or ethnicity, states, according to the Fourteenth Amendment, must provide compelling justification, and such justification must be rigorously examined.

The U. S. Supreme Court's Three-Tiered Approach

Over the decades, American courts have closely scrutinized legislative classifications under the Equal Protection Clause, and the Supreme Court has developed a three-tiered approach to examining the classifications. The first classification involves strict scrutiny in which the government must show that the classification in question (for example race, national origin, or religion) serves a compelling state interest and that the classification is necessary to serve that interest. The second classification involves middle-tier scrutiny in which the government must show that the classification in question (for example gender and sexual orientation) serves an important state interest and the classification is at least substantially related to serving that interest. The third and final classification involves minimum or rational scrutiny in which the government need only show that the classification in question (for example age) is rationally related to serving a legitimate state interest.

The application of a three-tiered approach by the courts in the implementation of the Equal Protection Clause reflects the court's desire to ensure balance and fairness in the administration of justice and the distribution of resources. The approach also recognizes that states and their functioning agents are not obligated to treat people the same. Various forces and contexts therefore may shape treatment. Herein lies the challenge. How does one know that one is being fair? And what treatment may constitute fair treatment? In a diverse society where race, ethnicity, gender, sexual orientation, disability, and so forth are constantly present in the dynamics of decision-making regarding the distribution of scarce resources, the nagging question among decision-makers has been how to relate to others and do one's work in a way that is perceived as fair. Most people would say that the solution is to treat everyone the same, and to follow the rules, whatever those rules are and regardless of who makes them and for what purpose. However, treating everyone the same and following the rules do not necessarily mean that one is being fair. Fairness is a much more complex process than that. Let me share a recent experience that demonstrates the complexity of this concept, the challenge of infusing it in public policy, and the need for clarity of thought in its application.

The California Stakeholders Group

In October 2001, the statewide Stakeholders Group appointed by former governor Gray Davis of California to redesign the state's child welfare system invited me to provide technical assistance to the group. Working with Judge Alice Lytle of the Superior Court of California and a small group of twenty individuals (part of the larger Stakeholders Group) drawn from both the private and public sectors, including neighborhood groups, my role was to provide leadership and guidance on how best to infuse fairness and equity throughout the emerging redesign efforts. To underscore how complex the concept of fairness is, I decided to engage workgroup members in a "pizza exercise." The pizza exercise was an activity my colleagues Don Taylor and Christine Wagner and I had developed several years earlier and had first used in our discussions on fairness issues at the Sacramento County Sheriff's Department. Using the same principles of the exercise, I created four groups at the Stakeholders project. Each group was then given 30 minutes to discuss and to come up with the fairest way to divide or share a 12-inch pizza among group members. The discussions that followed after the exercise were highly spirited, and brought out a range of varying dimensions around which each group constructed its perception of fairness in the division of the pizza. These dimensions are consistently present when decisions have to be made on how best to distribute or allocate resources that are increasingly scarce.

As the group demonstrated, decision outcomes on fairness typically focus on the following seven dimensions identified in the literature on organizational development:

> ➢ Equality—Some group members thought the fairest way was to divide the pizza equally, so that everyone has an equal chance of getting a slice. In other words, everyone should be treated the same. Recent conversations on the use of race in admission practices in our nation's law schools draw from this norm. Any suggestion of a different principle of fairness in admission practices is seen as discrimination.

> ➢ Need—Some group members wanted the pizza distributed to those who were hungriest; after all, they argued, these folks need the pizza the most. Conversations on the use of affirmative action in admission policies, resource allocation, hiring, and so forth that are based on the need to ensure diversity in these contexts grow out of this norm. Those opposed to this norm of

fairness call it reverse discrimination. The recent decision of the Supreme Court on the admission policy of the University of Michigan was based on the principle of need. I will return to this point later.

➢ Equity—Some group members insisted that the pizza be divided according to who contributed the most money for the pizza. Often, decisions about hiring, promotions, grades for class assignments, and so forth are based on this norm. Those who do the most work or make the most contribution to organizational productivity, the argument goes, should be rewarded.

➢ Seniority—Other group members suggested that the best way to divide the pizza was to have the oldest persons in the room get the slices first, with others getting what was left, if any. Sometimes, agencies make decisions based on this norm: promotion and training are sometimes based on who has the most seniority or those who have put in the most time. Many times, younger staff or those with higher expertise or qualifications, but are new to the organization, may resent this principle.

➢ Reciprocity—Let us take turns, argued some other members. Today let us give the pizza to Joe Sixpack; Jane Doe will have her turn next time. This norm of fairness involves taking turns, and we see it play out in various agencies with regard to how shifts, training, and so forth are scheduled.

➢ Chance—Let us draw out of a hat, and the lucky persons in the group get the pizza. This norm is ever-present in our lottery system—the paramount norm is luck.

➢ Choice—Finally, those who may not like pizza may elect to have none. It is their choice. These are individuals with dietary or other reasons.

From this exercise, it became clear that fairness is a very complex construct. How we perceive it varies, depending on the forces at stake. More importantly, fairness involves the application of selected norms, given certain conditions, regarding how we arrive at decisions. Thus, a crucial lesson from this exercise is that fairness is contextual. This is a very important characteristic that is always overlooked in our public discourse on fairness. Viewed from this perspective, fairness can be defined as a complex, contextual organizational and communication process in which different norms are applied in decision-making and resource allocation.

Those who exercise power therefore have tremendous discretion in what norms of fairness will apply in the decision-making process and public-policy framework. Those who exercise these powers thus have a responsibility to ensure that the process is perceived as consistent and impartial and that the rationale for the decisions made is fully explained.

Can We Truly Be Color-Blind?

For some Americans, the only way to be fair to all Americans is to be color-blind and to treat each other the same. This perspective of "a color-blind society" gained greater currency following the "I Have a Dream" speech of civil rights leader Dr. Martin Luther King, Jr. In that speech, King dreamed of a day when his four little children would be judged, "not by the color of their skin, but by the content of their character." It is this very ideal of a color-blind society that drove the Racial Privacy Initiative in California, championed by conservative University of California regent Ward Connerly and the California Republican Party, to eliminate racial identification on government forms in the state in Fall 2003. Underlying this ideal is the notion of fairness—to treat everyone the same. But this notion of fairness ignores the fundamental issue in King's message, fundamental principles of fairness embodied in our democratic experiment. In this regard, there is not a single norm for assessing fairness.

Thus had the citizens of California not rejected overwhelmingly the color-blind society initiative in October 2003, they would have dealt a serious blow to the ability of the state to address disparities in nearly every aspect of public life. Critical sources of information that the government has always used and relied upon for planning purposes and to ensure accountability would have been eliminated. More importantly, the government's ability to enforce anti-discrimination laws would have been significantly curtailed.

Supporters of the initiative argued that the racial categorization of people by the government represents one of the most divisive forces in American society, but their campaign failed to address important questions. How do we, for example, address disparities and patterns in educational opportunity and achievement, in diseases and healthcare, and in hate crimes and discrimination if we do not collect such vital demographic information related to race, ethnicity, and national origin? How do we plan and develop specific programs and strategies to deal with specific problems and challenges? However well intentioned, the Racial Privacy Initiative lacked common sense. It was divisive, deceptive, and distractive as well, and did little to enhance the dialogue on ways to move America beyond race.

The point is that building a color-blind society is not only impossible, but also undesirable. First, one must recognize that there is no such thing as being color-blind in a colorful society. We have always been a multicolored, multiracial society—a rainbow nation. And nothing is wrong with acknowledging that rich racial and cultural tapestry and using it for America's competitive advantage in a globalizing world. Second, the idea that being color-blind is being fair to all undermines the complex and contextual nature of the fundamental principles of fairness embodied in the Fourteenth Amendment to the Constitution. In our application of the law, we have always acknowledged mitigating circumstances in order to ensure fairness and balance. We must not shy away in applying it to the public policy arena.

Race and University Admission

President Bush's opposition to the use of race as a factor in college admission—precisely because he ignored the importance of acknowledging mitigating circumstances—was troubling. A narrow and strict conception of fairness (based only on the norm of equality) as defined in the president's position on admission processes, and that of many social conservatives, remains not only impractical, but also negates the basic principles and wisdom enshrined in the Equal Protection Clause. Clearly, given the norm of fairness based on need, the government has a compelling obligation to continue to use race as one of the criteria for collecting relevant data that help us to address disparities and patterns in education, health, diseases, hate crimes, and so forth. Furthermore, public institutions have a compelling obligation to continue to use race as one of the criteria for making admission decisions. This type of outreach ensures the kind of diversity that is critical to enriching the broad contours of knowledge and understanding in our nation's classrooms, and addresses serious gaps in educational opportunities for underrepresented groups in many fields where they are desperately needed. Consider for example, that 83 percent of the lawyers in California are white in a state where 53 percent of the population is nonwhite. Minority attorneys, according to a 2006 report of the State Bar, make up 17 percent of the lawyer population in the state.[16] We must do more to open the doors for more minorities in our law schools. The application of fairness requires care, understanding, and reason.

The University of Michigan Case

The Supreme Court was therefore right in its decision in 2003 regarding the admission policies at the University of Michigan Law School. The court ruled that diversity was a compelling state interest and that universities could use race as one of the criteria in making admission decisions in ways that open the door of opportunity to groups that had been historically denied such opportunity. Writing for the majority, Justice Sandra Day O'Connor said,

> As part of its goal of "assembling a class that is both exceptionally academically qualified and broadly diverse," the Law School seeks to "enroll a 'critical mass' of minority students." The Law School's interest is

not simply to "assure within its student body some specified percentage of a particular group merely because of its race or ethnic origin." That would amount to outright racial balancing, which is patently unconstitutional. Rather the Law School's concept of critical mass is defined by reference to the educational benefits that diversity is designed to produce. These benefits are substantial. As the District Court emphasized, the Law School's admissions policy promotes "cross-racial understanding," helps to break down racial stereotypes, and "enables (students) to better understand persons of different races." These benefits are "important and laudable," because "classroom discussion is livelier, more spirited, and simply more enlightening and interesting" when the students have "the greatest possible variety of backgrounds." The Law School's claim of compelling interest is further bolstered by its amici who point to the educational benefits that flow from student body diversity. ...Numerous studies show that student body diversity promotes learning outcomes and better prepares students for an increasingly diverse workforce and society, and better prepares them as professionals." These benefits are not theoretical, but real, as major American businesses have made clear that the skills needed in today's increasingly global marketplace can only be developed through exposure to widely diverse people, cultures, ideas, and viewpoints. What is more, high-ranking retired officers and civilian military leaders assert ... that a highly qualified, racially diverse officer corps is essential to national security.[17]

As Justice O'Connor noted, because universities, and in particular, law schools, represent the training ground for a large number of the nation's leaders, the path to leadership must be visibly open to talented and qualified individuals of every race and ethnicity. Thus, in the opinion of the Court, the Law School has a compelling interest in attaining a diverse student body.

However, the Supreme Court also noted that race-conscious admissions policies must be limited in time. In Justice O'Connor's words, "We take the Law School at its word that it would like nothing better than to find a race-neutral admissions formula and will terminate its race-conscious admissions program as soon as practicable. We expect that 25 years from now, the use of racial preferences will no longer be necessary to further the interest approved today."[18]

Indeed in making its decision on the use of affirmative action in admission processes, the Supreme Court reaffirmed an important principle of fairness: that context matters in deciding the complicated business of resource allocation, a point very often ignored in the fairness debate. Viewed more closely, the Court's decision was a rejection of the narrow and strict construction of fairness that is grounded on the norm of equality. The Court's decision was also a reaffirmation of the constitutionality of context, in this case the use of diversity in admission policies based on a specific norm of fairness that is grounded on need. This decision is in keeping with the letter and spirit of the Equal Protection Clause. Writes Justice O'Connor, "When race-based action is necessary to further a compelling governmental interest, such action does not violate the constitutional guarantee of equal protection so long as the narrow-tailoring requirement is also satisfied. Context matters when reviewing race-based governmental action under the Equal Protection Clause."[19] This decision was a major victory for those who have long believed that treating everyone the same may not always be fair and does very little to move our nation beyond race.

3

CLOSING THE CULTURE GAP IN AMERICA

Differences in interpersonal communication patterns both cause and result from cultural differences. Verbal communication systems, or languages, give each culture a common set of categories and distinctions with which to organize perceptions. These common categories are used to sort objects and ideas and to give meaning to shared experiences. Nonverbal communication systems provide information about the meanings associated with the use of space, time, touch, and gestures. They help to define the boundaries between members and nonmembers.

Myron Lustig and Jolene Koester

At the turn of the new century, we are wired, we are communicating, we are in some sense connected as never before. But the connections between us that are most meaningful, the everyday face-to-face human interactions that are the basis of community, have unmistakably eroded.

William R. Brody

We have learned much about the folly of excluding people on the presumption of ethnic/racial inferiority. But what we have not yet learned is how to make the process of Americanization work for all. I am not talking about requiring people to learn English or to adopt American ways; those things happen pretty much on their own. But as arguments about immigration heat up…, we also ought to ask some broader questions about assimilation, about how to ensure that people, once outsiders, don't forever remain marginalized within these shores.

Ellis Cose

Until Americans are willing to show a little more genuine curiosity about the joys and pains of one another's ethnic and racial experiences, we will continue to build walls between one another and true integration will continue to be nothing more than an elusive dream.

Clarence Page

Closing the Culture Gap in America

How else do we begin to construct the national dialogue on race? Living in California for more than a decade has made this question profound for me. California, as we know, is the nation's most populous state. Nearly thirty-four million people live here, representing about one-eighth of the nation's population. Perhaps the most diverse state in the union, with the nation's most racially integrated city, Sacramento, as its capital, California has an evolving demography that today is 47 percent white, with the remaining 53 percent consisting of ALANAs (African Americans, Latinos, Asians and Pacific Islanders, and Native Americans). This fact means that for the first time in the history of the state, Americans of European ancestry have become the minority. In addition, of the nearly thirty-four million people who live in the state, ten million are foreign-born. Students in its public schools speak 224 different languages drawn from the original nations of the citizens. It is now almost the norm to pick up the telephone, dial a business, and be prompted by a computer-activated voice to press a specific number to hear a message or speak with a customer service person in English or to press another number for another language. California's driver license instructions are now published in several of the major languages spoken in the state. Voter pamphlets are published in English and Spanish. Diversity is now, both in theory and practice, a fact in our public and social life.

If California were a nation, it would rank as the fifth largest economy in the world. A major Western gateway to the Pacific Rim, California trade offices are located in some of the major cities and regions across the globe with the sole purpose of engaging in commercial diplomacy and attracting investments to the state. California is also home to Silicon Valley, the world's technology beltway, and San Joaquin Valley, one of the nation's breadbaskets.

It also remains the nation's dominant economic engine, leading the country in science, technology, and innovation, and in entertainment, job creation, and venture capital funding, as well as other major growth industries. Because of the state's unique position and profile, managing diversity has become a critical strategic need.

If we accept the central premise that the American project for the twenty-first century is a dialogue of engagement in a nation of strangers and in a global community that is increasingly interconnected and economically interdependent, we must agree on two things: first, that managing differences as a strategic approach for moving beyond race and building an American community is central, and second, that managing differences as a strategic framework offers our nation a competitive advantage in a changing global marketplace.

The Three Commitments

At the least, the notion of managing differences provides a conceptual building block for reducing the gap in our understanding of each other. If we are convinced that building a strong American community can be enhanced through genuine dialogue, then managing diversity must be a paramount component of the new American project of understanding. Managing diversity requires a fundamental commitment to three things: a commitment to the philosophy of inclusion, a commitment to bridging the culture gap in America, and a commitment to fundamental principles of fairness, which I discussed in the previous chapter. How do we begin this project?

The Philosophy of Inclusion

First, we must re-examine our commitment to the philosophy of inclusion. In every institution of business, government, and social life, we must redouble our efforts to include people of diverse backgrounds and extend the opportunity of participation to those who have historically been excluded. It is a strange irony that one of the most venerable institutions of our government—the U. S. Senate—remains a club for mostly white men. And the Senate is not unique. The limited diversity among a group that makes laws for all of us raises questions regarding their sensitivity on matters of concern to all groups. The differing perceptions that underline America's continuing racial divide will not end unless all Americans—white, black, brown, red, oldtimers and newcomers, female and male—begin to feel a sense of equal opportunity to participate in all aspects of American life, including active participation at the highest levels of our halls of governance.

We know we are a nation of immigrants. We know that the very strength of the American character lies in its diversity. Our nation's history shows that America as we have come to know it has always been a heterogeneous society. Generations of American Indians resided here long before Spain's Christopher Columbus and Portugal's Amerigo Vespucci arrived from Europe. And there is now evidence that the first blacks sailed to this part of the world as free persons two hundred years before the beginning of the slave trade. Thus, we have always been a mixed society—a diverse nation. Moreover America, as a nation, has always been an evolving experiment, a nation steeped in adventure, risk-taking, and innovation. The essential pillars of American society crafted by the founding fathers—its style of democracy, the personal liberties, choice and free will, as well as private ownership of the means of production and distribution of goods and services typified by a competitive free market—remain enduring, but the American character, culture, and profile are ever-changing, a consequence of the nature of immigration at any given time in our nation's history.

At the beginning of the last century, we witnessed a large wave of new immigrants from Europe. Analysis of data from the U. S. Census Bureau shows that, of the nearly 9 million new immigrants who came to the U. S. in the early twentieth century, 89 percent came from Europe. By the end of the century, Latin America and Asia accounted for eight of the top 10 countries of origin for new immigrants in the United States.[20] We are witnessing today what some scholars have referred to as the largest wave of cultural mixing in human history, a consequence of the nation's changing demography. In this evolving cultural mosaic, every corner of our nation is drawing immigrants from Africa, Asia and the Pacific islands, Europe, Latin America and the Caribbean, as well as other distant corners from around the globe. The changing texture of the American character resulting from this evolving cultural mosaic is bound to affect, to some degree, the ways we live our lives and the ways we conduct business.

There is nothing new about this phenomenon. When racial and cultural groups come in contact with each other, nothing stays the same: something happens to the traditional ways we have done things in the past, and often, a new and better, more informed way of looking at reality emerges from this social intercourse. For instance, William Henry III, in a Time article entitled "Beyond the Melting Pot," argues that the "'browning of America' will alter everything in society from politics and education to industry, values and culture."[21] Clearly many Americans understand and see a value in America's form of diversity brought about by both voluntary and involuntary immigration. But others are concerned about the challenges of community building among peoples from differing racial and cultural groups. Speaking on the issue on the floor of Congress during a debate on immigration, Congressman Tom Tancredo echoed this sentiment:

> We're talking about something that goes to the very heart of this nation: whether or not we will actually survive as a nation. And here's what I mean by that. What we're doing here in this immigration battle is testing our willingness to actually hold together as a nation or split apart into

a lot of balkanized pieces. We are testing our willingness to actually hold on to something called the English language, something that is the glue that is supposed to hold us together as a nation. We are becoming a bilingual nation. And that is not good. And that is the fearful part of this. The ramifications are much, much more significant than any that we've been discussing so far.[22]

But a commitment to the philosophy of inclusion requires continual adjustment to the differences brought about by our evolving cultural mosaic. One cannot claim that he or she has a commitment to inclusion or that he or she places a value on diversity without some kind of cognitive reorientation. This kind of reorientation, informed by what it means to be an American, recognizes the need for continual adjustment to and flexibility toward cultural differences. This is the essential first step to moving beyond the acrimony on immigration and race, and to building an American community.

A genuine commitment to the philosophy of inclusion further recognizes that every American matters, that each American—black, white, brown, red, female and male, the oldtimer and the newcomer—is an integral part of the American fabric. Consider for example our educational system, where the curriculum has emphasized mostly the perspectives of white America. A commitment to the philosophy of inclusion requires teachers to incorporate American diversity and the different ways of knowing. No longer must our curricula focus on one group as reflecting the entire corpus of the American character and life. Preparing our students for interaction in a changing world requires exposure to cultural differences and variations in communication styles—one of the central challenges of the twenty-first century.

Accepting differences

While America's strength lies in its diversity, we also know that historically, accepting diversity has not always been an easy proposition for Americans. Writing in Newsweek about the current debate on immigration, Ellis Cose noted that "once again we are wondering whether we have too many of the wrong sort of newcomers" entering into our country, and likened the debate to the "days when Congress openly worried about inferior races polluting America's bloodstream."[23] For some, diversity goes contrary to their conception of the "American way of life." Attitudes that reflect this sentiment are plenty: "They're here now; they should speak English or go back to their country; they should do things the American way." "They are taking jobs away from us." "I want America to be for Americans, like it used to be." "People should know that this is America. When in Rome, do as the Romans do." But the very notion of "When in Rome" belies the fact that America is not Rome—a monocultural society. America is a diverse society. This much we know today. However, as Ellis Cose rightly notes, "we have learned much about the folly of excluding people on the presumption of ethnic/racial inferiority. But what we have not yet learned is how to make the process of Americanization work for all."[24]

At the height of the preparations to topple Iraqi president Saddam Hussein, one student narrated an experience at her work place when she told her workmates that she was opposed to going to war with Iraq. She said that a white colleague told her that she should go back to her country. This student, whose parents came to the U. S. as refugees from the war in Vietnam, had lost many family members. Therefore she understood the consequences of war, and spoke out from that perspective. Ironically, she was told to go back home by her colleague, who apparently failed to recognize that she was also an American citizen, who, like him, was born in California. In a broken voice, she recalled the experience and concluded that she felt terribly hurt by the ignorance of that remark.

Too many Americans go through similar experiences on a regular basis. And in times of crisis or periods of national emergency, the challenges are magnified. Negative stereotypes and prejudices increase. Telephone directories are used to ferret out names of suspected enemies. Anonymous telephone calls are made to these so-called enemies. Ethnic slurs are hurled at them. Vandalism and derogatory graffiti become commonplace. Hate crimes in the form of physical harassment go up. We may not know it, but for every negative act against persons we consider not one of us, we increase the dangers for our own people residing at home and abroad, and we paint America as an intolerant society.

In addition, those who are different from the majority are often considered inferior. Throughout my nearly two decades in America, I have noticed a troubling pattern in our discourse on differences. We view difference as a problem, a deficiency, and a liability. Until recently, industry, government, and education have devalued it. The result is limited career opportunities and low expectations of performance for those who are different. The common approach to difference has been to require those who are different to assimilate, to strive to fit in, to be more like the dominant or majority culture. Embedded in this approach is the belief that everyone should be treated in the same manner. Nothing should be done systemically and systematically to incorporate difference.

While we have made some progress towards expanding opportunities, the assimilationist model, a model that relies on changing cultural behaviors to the extent that it enhances task performance rather than relationships and people skills, unfortunately remains the practice for many businesses in America. Ali Mazrui of the Institute of Global Cultural Studies at Binghamton University in New York summarizes it this way: "Whereas the United States has been the greatest asylum for diverse peoples, it has not been the greatest refuge for diverse cultures. The doors of transcultural communication have seldom been kept wide open in U. S. policy."[25] A new dialogue of engagement requires opening the doors of transcultural communication.

Managing differences

What else must we do? A real commitment to the philosophy of inclusion recognizes there is a cost associated with managing differences. It is not enough to open the doors of the world of work to women, celebrating our diversity in the workplace, while at the same time refusing to make provisions for those things that create a comfortable work environment for women. It is not enough to open the doors of the world of work to those who are physically challenged, proclaim that we value diversity, while at the same time refusing to invest in access or those things that make the workplace comfortable for people who are physically challenged. It is not enough for a corporation to say that it values a diverse customer base, while at the same time refusing to invest in an equally diverse staff in ways that serve those customers more efficiently. A genuine commitment to the philosophy of inclusion must be accompanied with the astute understanding that managing diversity costs money, but ultimately the expenditure increases productivity and efficiency. For too long, Americans have claimed to value diversity while ignoring and perhaps not understanding the cost dimension associated with it. It is time for corporate and governmental America to walk the walk and not just talk the talk.

Related to this commitment is the need to confront lingering systemic issues about racial preferences in such areas as hiring and employment practices, promotion and disciplinary policies, and contracting services, among others. These issues are at the core of the racial divide. It is no longer enough to say that one values diversity without demonstrating in practical terms and specific contexts how this value for diversity manifests itself. Too often I have heard managers in agencies make the claim that they value diversity. When probed further to identify specific contexts that show this, most of these managers are only able to point to cultural events and festivities that they have held at their offices. However, valuing diversity is not all about cultural celebrations and getting together to sing "kumbaya" and eat sushi. Valuing diversity is a multifaceted process involving a series of action steps that helps to move an individual and the organization from awareness of cultural differences to understanding, acceptance, appreciation, and respect for these differences. While the kinds of activities that managers often talk about increase awareness about diversity, they are not enough to move individuals and the organization strategically to higher levels of cultural competency and growth. Where diversity is placed in the organization's list of strategic priorities and what action steps are designed to implement these priorities are fundamental to understanding whether the organization values diversity. Today's organizational leaders cannot claim that they value diversity when the profile of the manager's workplace does not reflect diversity, and when there is no evidence of affirmative effort[26] to make the workplace reflective of the profile of the community. More importantly, organizational leaders must recognize that the mere presence of diversity in the workplace is not enough to guarantee positive outcomes. To improve the quality of organizational processes and outcomes, the presence of diversity in an organization must be coupled with a long-term systematic program for effectively managing diversity. A growing body of research on small-group communication provides support for this view.[27]

Let me speak now on the concept of affirmative effort. Affirmative effort requires organizations and their leaders to make proactive efforts, in the absence of affirmative action laws, to diversify their workplaces. The fact that affirmative action has been banned in such states as California does not make meaningless the application of affirmative effort to make the workplace look like America. When President Clinton took office in January 1993, he kept his campaign promise that he would make his cabinet look like America. He named the first female secretary of state in U. S. history, Madeleine Albright, a former professor of law at Georgetown University. He named several minorities to his cabinet, Ron Brown, Hazel O'Leary, Mike Espy, (all African Americans), and Norman Mineta, the first Asian American to serve at the highest level of the U. S. government. Mineta was transportation secretary in President George W. Bush's cabinet. Indeed President Bush has followed in Clinton's footsteps. Today, Dr. Condoleeza Rice, an African American, is America's second female Secretary of State. Madeleine Albright (appointed by President Clinton) was the first female Secretary of State. Rice was the nation's first female national security advisor. General Colin Powell was the first African American to hold the office of Secretary of State. By Constitutional provision, the holder of this office is the fourth-highest-ranking member of the U. S. government, after the president, the vice president, and the speaker of the House. If the first three become incapacitated, the Secretary of State would automatically become the president of the United States. These appointments suggest the nature of the progress that we have made since our democratic experiment began more than two hundred years ago. However, just as it is normal and ordinary news to have white males occupy such positions, so too should it be for women and other racial groups in our country to occupy such positions. We cannot move beyond race until such appointments are no longer extraordinary news in America. And we must not wait for incapacitation to occur before fellow Americans from racial minorities and women of all races dream of occupying the highest office in our land. We cannot move beyond race until all groups begin to feel that they are Americans. The fact that the top two candidates for the Democratic party presidential primaries were African American (Senator Barack Obama) and female (Senator Hilary Clinton), and the progress we have seen in the nomination of Senator Obama and Governor Sarah Palin on the top two tickets of the two major political parties in our country speaks highly of the nation's efforts to move beyond race and gender. Now is the time to match our rhetoric of commitment to the philosophy of inclusion with action. Managing the demands and expectations brought about by diversity remains the single greatest task of our society and today's workplace.

Bridging the Culture Gap

The second fundamental requirement for managing our country's differences is a commitment to bridging the culture gap in America. If the nature and quality of the present dialogue on race relations in this country are yardsticks for measurement of our knowledge of each other, one does not need to be convinced about the presence of a culture gap in America. Ask many Americans of differing ancestries to share with you what they know of each other, and you will probably get a blank response. A recent meeting with former state assemblyman Dennis Mangers, now senior vice president of California Cable Association, and prominent Sacramento attorney Joe Ginshlea, now chair of the American Leadership Forum, highlighted further the complexity of this question. Mangers's roots draw from a combination of several European backgrounds, Ginshlea is of Irish ancestry, and I am originally from Nigeria. All three of us are American citizens—the first two by birth, myself through naturalization. We had come together that afternoon to brainstorm some strategies and practices for best incorporating a dialogue on diversity in the context of the leadership programs of the American Leadership Forum (ALF). ALF was founded in 1980 in Texas by Joe Jaworski "to offer a new leadership model for addressing the complex problems facing our society."[28] It is a national non-profit organization dedicated to revitalizing leadership within communities across the nation. Working with leaders who run businesses, shape public policy and manage organizations, ALF provides an opportunity that helps these leaders to build trusting relationships with each other, and to develop skills in collaboration that can be applied to benefit the community. The idea behind ALF is that as the network of bonded leaders grows, so too does its potential to bring about positive and constructive change.

As we talked on the fourth floor of the historic Senator Hotel (now an office complex), about how best to broach the subject of diversity within ALF, our conversation touched on our backgrounds and some of the people we have worked with from diverse backgrounds. It became increasingly clear that we were not really familiar with those we claimed to know. In reality, the folks we go out with for dinner are generally those who are like us and who share the same interests. To the extent that they are not like us, we may know of them, but we do not really know them. The challenge of diversity, remarked Mangers, is to go the extra mile to forge new friendships beyond our racial and ethnic comfort zones, and to create strategies for assessing progress. This challenge requires leadership.

The question posed by Nation of Islam leader Minister Louis Farrakahn at the Million Family March held in Washington, D.C. a few years ago further highlights the deficiency in our knowledge of each other: What do we know of each other, but the worst of each other? Indeed, a central reality of American life is that our knowledge of other races is poor. If we are to build an American community, we must first acknowledge this gap. We must accept the elementary fact that we know little of each other and move away from our denial of the existence of a culture gap in our society.

What do I mean by a culture gap? A culture gap exists when an individual from one racial or ethnic group lacks knowledge of the cultural patterns, attitudes, and communication styles of another racial or ethnic group. Such lack of knowledge may lead to fear and suspicion of one another; it may also lead us to think the worst of each other; it may lead to misunderstanding, prejudice, stereotypes, misperceptions, and faulty attribution of motives. It may also lead to a breakdown in communication. Thus culture gap is synonymous with knowledge gap. While awareness of our diversity may be high among most sectors of American society, there is a huge gap in our knowledge of the cultural patterns and communication styles of the various groups, which make up our society. Our conversations on race, because they remain polarized, have had no positive impact in bridging the knowledge gap between the various groups in our society. A fundamental task of the twenty-first century, if we truly want to move beyond race, must be to bridge this gap. In addition, knowledge of the cultural backpacks of fellow Americans also helps us to understand our own cultural backpacks and possibly why we act the way we do. Such growth provides enormous potential for individual change.

Bridging the culture gap in America requires us to change the way we think about our own understanding of diversity. Many Americans tend to assume that because they live in neighborhoods that are diverse, they know everything there is to know about the subject. I have conducted numerous workshops on diversity, and every now and then a person claims that he or she does not need this workshop because "as a minority, I have had to deal with white people all my life. They are the ones that need to be here." Nine times out of ten, I hear this statement from African American participants. While some of us have dealt with various groups, (including white people) all of our lives, and live even today in communities and neighborhoods that are diverse, the fact is that our lives remain separate and disconnected from the lives of our neighbors. Living in a diverse neighborhood does not necessarily mean one is diverse or that one is multicultural. Being diverse or multicultural is both an attitude and a way of life. It is a state of mind where inclusion is central to one's thinking. Such a mindset must form part of the strategy for the new dialogue of engagement.

In 1997, I led a team of consultants at the request of a major public agency in the country to conduct cultural diversity training for over one thousand staff members in eight locations scattered throughout the country. What struck me during one of the training sessions was the remark of a white woman in the audience following a debriefing of one of the exercises. The exercise was designed to have participants take an introspective look at themselves, and to assess how monocultural or multicultural they were on a scale of 1 though 10, with 1 being most monocultural and 10 being more multicultural. For most of the participants, it became clear that the more they moved away from their monocultural beginnings to the world of work, the more they found themselves in multicultural settings. But being in a multicultural setting, argued the young woman, did not mean that one has mastered the tools for navigating such environment. Living or working in a multicultural setting does not mean that one is multicultural, she contended. "Who do I call when I have problems or need help?" she continued. "I live in a diverse neighborhood," she confessed, "but who do I interact with in my neighborhood? I am sorry to say it, but my white friends. I have not ventured out of my comfort zone to initiate new friendships with those who do not look like me." Clearly, many of us, if we care to tell the truth, are like this woman. We have taken up residences in multicultural communities, but in reality, we are still very monocultural. How can we address long-standing cultural and racial stereotypes if we do not talk to one another? How can we address our mutual fears if we do not visit each other, have bread together or have tea together? How can we bridge the culture gap if we are on the outside looking in?

We must also admit we have done very little to promote cross-cultural understanding and improve human relations in our domestic arena. The investment in strengthening people's skills, or what some refer to as emotional intelligence, in our public and private sector environments is ludicrous when compared to the thousands of dollars devoted to strengthening technical capacities in such areas as computer skills. One principal of an elementary school told me in a recent conversation that the annual budget for human relations skills training for staff members in his school was only three hundred dollars—and we wonder why the culture gap would remain in that school. The implications for teaching and learning in a school whose student population is diverse or not diverse can be staggering. How do the teachers, for example, navigate the challenges and dynamics of increasingly multicultural classrooms and improve intercultural communication in that context? How do they deal with issues of pedagogy, learning styles, and curriculum in their classrooms in ways that reflect our nation's evolving demography? These are important questions. Without the resources to prepare our teachers to deal with the emerging challenges from the new demography, the students we produce will know very little about the peoples of America, about the world, and about one another's cultural patterns and communication styles, and will be able to contribute little to the larger society. The prospects are frightening for a twenty-first century multicultural

America and a world, given the present nature of global commerce and international relations that is more interdependent than ever.

I am afraid to say that we are at the crossroads of cultural ignorance in American society. One could add that this cultural ignorance extends to our knowledge about the rest of the world. In 2002, National Geographic and Roper released a fascinating report of their survey of the global knowledge of American youth. Notice how our young citizens performed in the following table:

WHERE IN THE WORLD?
[among 18-24-year-old Americans given maps]
87 percent cannot find Iraq
83 percent cannot find Afghanistan
76 percent cannot find Saudi Arabia
70 percent cannot find New Jersey
49 percent cannot find New York
11 percent cannot find the United States

Source:

http://archives.cnn.com/2002/education/11/20/geography.quiz/ (accessed May 18, 2008).

In virtually all global literacy tests, our students generally perform below the international average of their peers in other highly industrialized countries. Acknowledging this problem, former education secretary Roderick Paige remarked, "It's a world of 24-hour news cycles, global markets, high-speed Internet and big challenges. ... And in order for our children to be prepared to take their place in that world and rise to those challenges, they must first understand it."[29]

The new American project of the twenty-first century requires both public and private investments in human capital related to people's skills—in our capacities to understand each other and the world around us in a way that gives us competitive advantage in an increasingly interdependent global market. The maintenance of U. S. influence in a single-superpower world certainly must be coupled with cultural knowledge of distant places that are linked to our continuing prosperity, peace, and security. Central to this project is intercultural competence.

Myron Lustig at San Diego State University and Jolene Koester at California State University, Northridge define culture as "a learned set of shared interpretations about beliefs, values, norms, and social practices, which affect the behaviors of a relatively large group of people."[30] Inherent in this definition is that culture has an internal dimension, the deep structure, and an external dimension, the surface structure. Thus such things as beliefs, values, experiences, and attitudes are constitutive elements of the deep structures of a culture. We do not wear them on our faces. We cannot see them, and those around us do not see them either. Yet the deep structures are powerful enough to shape the surface structures of human behavior: our behaviors and actions, our words, how we work, how we dress, what we eat, how we construct courtship and marriage, our gift-giving habits, how we mourn, celebrate, and bury the dead, how we adorn ourselves, how we relate to nature, how we relate to others, and how we perceive the world around us—in sum, how we communicate and live.

Both the deep and surface structures reflect our culture, and what I call cultural backpacks. In these backpacks are our values, beliefs, attitudes, and norms. Our membership in one racial group—whether one is Negroid, Caucasoid, Mongoloid—or our ethnicities—whether one is Irish, Italian, Polish, German, Serb, Igbo, Hausa, Zulu, Aztec, Jewish, or Arab—are shaped by a shared sense of a common culture, and this common culture produces a preferred style of communicating with other people. When we ignore this fact, we experience culture bumps, and often we attribute these bumps to other things. Culture bumps can be likened to a head-on collision between two vehicles, in this case between two individuals with differing cultural backpacks (i.e., differing cultural backgrounds or world orientations). A culture bump may occur when there is a cultural disconnect between two culturally different individuals to the degree that the bumps result in a communication breakdown.

Our primary schools must constitute the starting points for the discourse on culture and its impact on our behavior. We live in a nation of strangers, but we can understand our strangeness and turn it into productive energy when we make a genuine investment in our educational system to bridge the culture gap. Our high schools must be involved in this process as well. Intercultural understanding must also be central in the curriculum for undergraduate education. Our citizens should be grounded in the people skills needed for successfully navigating a twenty-first-century world.

A Word about Diversity Training

Let me take a moment to talk about cultural diversity and sensitivity training. A number of public and private agencies have adopted this approach as their way of managing differences and bridging the culture gap. In recent years, people have told me that diversity training reminds us too much of our differences, that it is much too divisive, that it puts people on the defensive and makes everyone feel uncomfortable. In fact, one woman from a state agency wrote me a letter some years ago expressing those fears and concerns when I was invited to conduct a pre-training assessment of diversity issues in her organization. Others have told me that it is counter-productive because it makes them feel guilty, especially when they believe they have not been a part of the problem. My response has always been the same. Any climate of fear or concern expressed in the manner that I have described regarding diversity training suggests a very urgent need for diversity training.

Diversity, by its very nature, produces great discomfort, at least initially. Similarity minimizes the degree of discomfort. But the discomfort produced by diversity, if properly harnessed, leads to personal growth. I must also add that any climate of fear or concern stated in the manner that I have described above also suggests a myopic understanding of the broad nature of diversity. I will return to this point in a moment.

If done well, one need not feel troubled about diversity training. The problem, however, with diversity training is that it has been conducted by many who have no knowledge of what they are doing, nor any knowledge of the best way to proceed. Perhaps this situation explains why there is a negative perception of diversity training. In reality, having unqualified individuals conducting diversity training makes bridging the culture gap more difficult. It is like going to a dentist rather than a doctor to fix your back problems. We find ourselves facing the same problem with journalism practice today: many men and women who have no training in journalism parade themselves as reporters and report for news organizations. They have no training in the essential requirements for objective reporting, except in so far as they have a degree or diploma in some field. They add their views on what is supposedly a news story. They become the news and the news becomes their views. They editorialize. Tough questions are not asked of our leaders. They have substituted press freedom with the freedom to praise, becoming the lapdogs of government, instead of its watchdogs. Men like Bill O'Reilly, Brit Hume, Sean Hannity, Tony Snowe, Geraldo Rivera, and even Wolf Blitzer are examples. They continue to do a disservice to journalism, just as personality cults and fly-by-nighters do a disservice to the diversity industry.

The absence of trained professionals conducting diversity training is compounded also by the fact that there is no set of guidelines regarding content area and praxis, i.e., what to incorporate and how to design and deliver the material. The result is a growing industry peopled with personalities, a cult of well-known persons from minority groups, who, because of their experience with racism and discrimination, believe that they are now qualified to provide diversity training. Many agencies, having no choice or not knowing what to draw from, buy into the cult and pay lots of money to the big names for a paltry presentation that does more harm than good. With training that focuses only on race, the audience is left with a sad commentary about our racial problems, but not a set of best practices regarding the broad and complex nature of diversity, how one can grow in cultural competency, or how one can continue to grow, and what an agency can do to measure progress, long after the personality has gone. For many agencies, diversity training, like sexual harassment training, has become a one-shot affair, designed to protect the agency from potential lawsuits and citizen complaints.

A related problem, one that I have also found gravely troubling, is the perception in some agencies and among some minority group members that only those who are persons of color can deliver diversity training. Such thinking automatically disqualifies a white trainer. Those who make this case suggest that a white person has not walked in their shoes and therefore "cannot understand our issues or how we feel." Consequently, such an individual, in their view, cannot conduct diversity training. There is something fundamentally dubious in this argument. First, it suggests a very narrow conception of diversity in the sense that the trainer is coming to an agency only to address "our issues." Second, it elevates the "us vs. them" syndrome in an agency, as a cadre of potentially qualified people from a racial group is eliminated from the training pool because of a terribly weak argument grounded on skin color. Third, it creates resentment within an agency as white employees think the training is targeted only toward them. The opportunity for growth for everyone is then lost in the process. On both sides of the aisle, minorities and white employees have shared these concerns with me.

The same criterion is sometimes extended to new immigrants: one cannot do diversity training because the "person doesn't understand our history," the argument goes. A few years ago, I became a victim of these same concerns when I was almost denied the opportunity to provide diversity and racial sensitivity training for a major California state agency. Certain community leaders from the African American community had expressed reservations that as a native-born African, I might not be able to provide training for this troubled agency because I had not walked in their shoes. I had been told by the agency that I was the most qualified for the work, and therefore the administrators refused to bow down to community pressure. It was a very exasperating experience, to say the least, but weeks of negotiations resolved the matter in my favor. The training curriculum was designed after a comprehensive needs assessment of the agency, and it was delivered to several hundred staff persons. Nearly 95 percent of them evaluated the training as very good to excellent, and also indicated in the impact assessment conducted six months later that their knowledge level had "increased" or "substantially increased." It seems to me, given my expertise and experience as a consultant on this subject, that one's preparation, not race or ethnicity, should be the deciding criterion for selecting who ultimately does diversity training for an agency. The politics of color that has surrounded diversity training since its inception must now give way to specific trainer academic qualifications and cultural competencies that are crucial to designing a systematic and sustainable program on diversity for both individual and organizational growth within an agency.

Race is important in our conversations on diversity. Race, however, is not the quintessential identifier of diversity. Most people who express fear about diversity and others who provide training in it generally focus on race. It ought to be clear to all Americans now that American diversity, the very strength of our nation, is multifaceted. American diversity, informed by both forced and voluntary immigration, is a mixed profile that includes race, ethnicity, gender, generational differences, socio-economic status, physical abilities, sexual orientation, marital status, medical conditions, and much more. Understanding the many elements of this rich profile and the ramifications for communication and human relations is the focus of diversity training. The new American project of understanding must embrace diversity training in toto, with communication as the glue that holds the conversation.

Unfortunately, in conducting diversity training, the trend for many trainers and agencies has been to focus only on attitudinal issues such as prejudice, stereotypes, racism, and discrimination. This focus appears to have shaped the climate of fear and concern about the goals and outcomes of diversity training. Few trainers or specialists and agencies focus on cultural patterns and communication styles. Diversity training is not only about attitudes. It is also about cultural patterns and communication styles. The critical challenge is to recognize that addressing all three of these issues— attitudes, cultural patterns, and communication styles—are material to bridging the culture gap in America.

The new American project of understanding must go beyond training and should include efforts to immerse ourselves in the experiences of other cultures. This kind of immersion involves looking beyond the confines of one's race, one's ethnicity, and one's culture. As my colleagues and I noted in an earlier work, many of us "live as prisoners of our own cultures and feel bound to act and think in total agreement with their presumptions and teachings, no matter how narrowly defined they may be."[31] The notion of becoming transcultural requires genuine dialogue and interaction with other cultural groups. It is through this process that one can understand and affirm "diverse ways of knowing, communicating, and behaving, so that when individuals from different cultures come together, there is the potential for each to be enriched by the other...."[32]

The New Segregated Hour in America

Martin Luther King Jr., at the dawn of the modern civil rights movement, lamented that "We must face the fact that in America, the church is still the most segregated major institution in America. At 11:00 on Sunday morning when we stand and sing, ... We stand at the most segregated hour in this nation. This is tragic."[33] And the first way the church "can move out into the arena of social reform," notes King, "is to remove the yoke of segregation from its own body."[34] King's indictment, write Ron Stodghill and Amanda Bower in Time magazine, "still carries weight today, as an estimated 90 percent of Americans worship primarily with members of their race or ethnicity."[35] But Stodghill and Bower suggest that, given America's evolving complex social tapestry, segregation in our nation's churches may not be driven by bigotry, but by language barriers and cultural heritage.

Maybe they are right. But we have also not bridged the segregation in many areas of our public and social life, especially in one area where I had hoped we had made progress—in the nation's workplaces and schools. As I observe the cultural landscape in my travels, I am struck with what I have come to see frequently as commonplace in America's diners and restaurants. It now seems to me that the second most segregated hour in our country is the noon lunch hour at workplaces and schools across America. While people from diverse backgrounds now work and go to school together in an integrated environment, when it comes to lunchtime, they choose to go in different directions—with those who look like them. It is not clear whether segregation at lunch times is driven by bigotry or by language barriers and cultural heritage.

I am concerned that we have turned our workplaces and schools into places to perform tasks only, at the expense of strengthening relationships between various groups. Both task performance and building and maintaining relations are crucial to bridging the gap between people, and in building trust and ultimately a strong community. How can we know the person we work with or go to school with if we do not take the time to get to know the person? We must break the cycle of segregation that has enveloped our nation by engaging in activities that immerse us in each other's experiences.

I am convinced that immersing ourselves in the experiences of other groups can go a long way toward bridging the culture gap in America. Yes, our lives are busy, but we can take up the challenge of visiting a black church on Sunday for service or a Buddhist temple in our neighborhood. We can participate in the Irish celebration of St. Patrick's Day or immerse ourselves in the Latino celebration of Cinco de Mayo. We can view the Native American celebration of pow-wow or an East Indian wedding, the German Oktoberfest, the Jewish Hanukkah, the African American Kwanzaa. One does not necessarily have to come from the groups that organize or host these events to be a part of them. Certainly, groups who organize these events should extend invitations to other groups who may feel unwelcome, or who may feel that their presence might be perceived as a violation. Diversity as an attitude and a way of life requires motivation, encouragement, and practice. Invariably along the way, one may experience varying degrees of discomfort or stress in interactions with those who are different. But only through such interactions can comfort and personal growth result.

Finally, as we begin the new dialogue of engagement, we must remember that we bring "stuff" to our communication with others. We bring our cultural backpacks, our assumptions about what is right and wrong. These assumptions impact the decisions we make, the ways we negotiate meaning, and the nature and quality of communication we have. The stuff we bring to communication is shaped by our many differences. We are different because our ancestries and cultures are different; our histories, our upbringing, and our ways of life are different. Our communication styles are different because our cultures have shaped them.

Understanding these differences leads us to the fundamental realization that those differences are not about right or wrong. These differences only reflect other valid ways of looking at reality. The fact that one comes from a minority or majority culture does not make one's culture right or wrong. We cannot bridge the culture gap in America unless we understand these conditions. We must understand them in ways that allow us to recognize that we are bound together as a nation by an inescapable garment of destiny, a common hope in the greatness of our diversity, and a shared vision of an American community. Either we learn how to live together, or we choose to tear each other apart.

4

COMING TO AMERICA:
NEWCOMERS IN A NEW SOCIETY

We must be one as neighbors, as fellow citizens, not separate camps, but families—white, black … all of us, no matter how different, who share basic American values and are willing to live by them … Whether we like it or not, we are one nation, one family, indivisible, and for us, divorce or separation are not options.

President Bill Clinton

The whole barrier exists because most people never come together and sit down at a table … join together, break bread together, and celebrate their differences and their likenesses.

Oprah Winfrey

It is one thing to throw people from different worlds together in a classroom or an Army boot camp and yet another thing to make them feel a connection that produces a sense of community and mutual commitment. More is needed than proximity.

Christopher Edley, Jr.

To effectively navigate and manage differences, one must have a fundamental shift in worldview—from one that says: my village is the world, to that which says: the world is my village.

Ogom P. Nwosu

In its regular account about the state of international education,[36] the Institute of International Education reported a significant increase in the number of international students who come to the U. S. to participate in American higher education. In the period 2001–2002, more than 582,000 international students were enrolled in American universities and colleges representing a 6.4 percent jump from the numbers reported in 1980. More than 55 percent of these students came from Asia, 14 percent from Europe, 11.7 percent from Latin America, 6.6 percent from the Middle East, 6.6 percent from Africa, and 5.4 percent from North America and Oceania. Following a two-year decline in enrollment, the number of international students at U.S. universities "remained steady at 564,766 in 2005/06."

International students complement current sources of traditional enrollment in American universities and colleges, and they serve as an important funding source for U. S. higher education and the national economy. In the years 2000 and 2001, international students spent nearly $12 billion on tuition and living expenses, including support for accompanying family members. Data from the U. S. Department of Commerce describes U. S. higher education as the country's fifth largest service-sector export.[37]

International students join a growing number of new immigrants who come to the U. S. each year. In the past four years alone, four million new immigrants came to the U. S., bringing the total number of foreign-born residents in the country to an all-time high of 34.2 million, according to an analysis by the Center for Immigration Studies of the most recent numbers from the Census Bureau.[38] Between 1990 and 2001, immigrants accounted for more than half of the growth in the U. S. labor force. Clearly, the presence of new immigrants contributes to the strengthening of our understanding of global issues, helps to eliminate hostile preconceptions, promotes intercultural relations, and improves the opportunities for peace and development around the world.

Newcomers to America's shores come for various reasons. Some seek to escape the economic and political hardships in their country and to find a better life in America. Others are here because of the desire to change residences or to have multiple residences. Some are international businesspeople, diplomats, foreign students, migrant and exchange workers, or tourists. They come from different countries across the globe and from all walks of life. The newcomers represent America's newest strangers. While the general impression is that many are poor, others in fact come from backgrounds of comfort.

New immigrants bring with them cultural attributes that are different, at least in some sense, from those attributes that are valued by the people they encounter in their host locations. Thus, they must face the prospect of negotiating new identities and adjusting to the host location in order to become not just functional but also a part of the American community. Many succeed in doing so. For some, the challenges of adjustment compel them to withdraw from participation in the larger community. The result is the emergence of Korea Towns, Chinatowns, Little Italies, and other little communities across the nation that provide support to the new members of their communities. The danger is that these communities of support may become communities of isolation, making it harder for newcomers to become a part of the American community. What are the challenges involved in adapting to the U. S., and what must new immigrants do to become a part of the American community?

Some years ago, I shared some of my experiences going through this process in an article entitled "Cultural Problems and Intercultural Growth: My American Journey."[39] With permission, I am providing a revised version of the same article here. My goal is to offer a useful primer for newcomers in their adjustment processes in the U. S. But the oldtimers have a responsibility to assist the newcomers in building a truly genuine American community.

Coming to America

In 1985, I left Nigeria for the U. S. on an educational scholarship. I had been offered a graduate fellowship by Nigeria's Federal Agricultural Coordinating Unit, a World Bank-assisted unit charged with the responsibility of coordinating all of the Bank's integrated rural development projects in the country. The fellowship was to enable me to pursue graduate studies with a specialization in communication and instructional media technology at Towson State University, Baltimore, part of the University System of Maryland and a predominantly European American institution.

I was to proceed later to the mainly African American Howard University in Washington, D.C. to pursue doctoral work in human communication studies, with emphasis in communication processes across cultures. My mother, Cecilia, recognized as the matriarch of the family, had organized a reception in keeping with family tradition, and had invited several people to bid me farewell. As the entirety of my family and friends gathered, little did they realize that I would probably be spending quite some years in the U. S. Most foreign students to the U. S. initially come to study, only to find themselves settling in the country upon the completion of their studies. For many, the political, economic, and cultural realities in their countries of origin compel them to seek ways to remain abroad. Before they realize it, time has passed by. And they see themselves staying five more years, ten years, fifteen years, twenty years. With marriage, and children, and family, it becomes increasingly difficult to return home. America is now their new home, and they must juggle the challenges, requirements, and promises of this new home with the longing to return to the original home that they left many years ago. This juggling act between the new and the old prevents newcomers to the U. S. from genuine participation in building an American community.

My arrival at Dulles International Airport near Washington, D.C. on September 19, 1985 was tainted with mixed feelings and perceptions. On one hand, I had great excitement and curiosity about a land I had been told flowed with milk and honey. And the things I saw upon arrival seemed to confirm that impression: the magnificence of the airport infrastructure, the huge paved roads, the numerous high-rise buildings, and the lighted streets. It was as if the roads had been swept. Yet in the midst of this grandeur, I had flashbacks of stories I had been told of race relations in the U. S. I had flashbacks of negative images of blacks portrayed on Nigerian television, images of the buffoonish behavior of J. J. in the old television sitcom Good Times, images of blacks in subservient or supporting roles. Those images heightened my initial fears about living in the U. S., and I wondered about the opportunities for a person of my background. I also wondered about the nature of the relationships that would emerge between my African American relatives and myself.

I left Nigeria with the impression that the African American was confined to a life of silliness and crime in America, and that the experience of slavery had wrought considerable havoc on the psyche of blacks. My experiences in Nigeria with some African Americans living and working in Nigeria did little to change or alter the very negative perceptions reflected in media images which had become the prism through which I saw life in America. My initial interactions with African Americans upon arrival in the U. S. were therefore filled with both curiosity, because I wanted to get to know them, and fear, because of the negative portrayals. Such fear was manifested in my polite refusal to accept an offer from a young African American male staffer who had asked to assist me with my luggage at Dulles

International Airport. Yet I found myself feeling safe when the same offer came moments later from a Caucasian male attendant.

New Americans and Media Images

For most newcomers to a foreign land, including the U. S., their knowledge of a place is typically informed by media images. Clearly, the distorted depictions of blacks in the American mass media to which we had access in Nigeria helped condition my perceptions of and relationship with the group upon arrival in the U. S. Those perceptions were to change by the time I went to study at Howard University for my doctorate. And they changed because I offered myself the opportunity to interact with people of African American background. If we are to move beyond our distorted perceptions of other groups in American society, and participate in building an American community, we must engage them. We must interact with them. We must talk with them. We must learn about them. The American project of the twenty-first century requires such engagement.

Culture Bumps and Communication Failures

At Towson State University in Maryland I continued my American journey. A predominantly white institution, located on a pristine campus, Towson had more than sixteen thousand students. There, I found myself the only black face or one of the very few black faces in several of my classes and on the campus. I had never been exposed to such a sea of white faces in my life. Here I encountered some of the initial culture bumps. For me, the bumps came in many shapes and sizes.

The first was the issue of the English language. In my initial interactions with U. S. Americans born here, there were difficulties related to use of verbal and nonverbal codes, including the meanings assigned to various actions or behaviors. One such difficulty arose during my encounter with snow. I had never seen snow in my life until I came to the U. S. There is no word in my Igbo language[40] for it either. Cultures essentially create names for what exists in their environments. My knowledge of snow came from watching television and classroom discussions about other societies at St. Mary's Elementary School in Enugu, Nigeria. The teacher would liken snow to ice formations in one's refrigerator. For someone who has not experienced snow, that description in and of itself does not capture the phenomenon. My sister had warned me of the need to be careful during winter since large tracks of snow tend to turn into ice.

On one particular morning in Baltimore I woke up to the sight of snow and clearly was enthused by it. My college friend, Sam, who is African American, joined me at my apartment residence as I prepared for school that morning. A few minutes later, we both left the apartment walking down the stairwell, which had been partially covered by snow. Not remembering my sister's warning, I watched myself slip and roll down to the bottom of the stairwell. I was in great pain. I expected that my friend would say that he was sorry about the incident and assist in lifting me up from the ground. Rather, he kept asking, "Are you alright? Are you alright?" The more he asked the question, the angrier I became. When I finally managed to get up on my own, I wasted no time in telling him how inconsiderate he was. Sam could not understand why I would expect him to say "sorry" when he was not responsible for my fall. Years later at Howard University when I had to reprocess that interaction, it became clear that our remarks regarding appropriate behaviors and linguistic norms were a function of our cultural backpacks. It was an interesting awakening that culture matters. Clearly, the culture gap in our knowledge of each other created the culture bumps and the communication breakdown.

Among Africans, regardless of the circumstances, it is appropriate for the person present to indicate his or her sympathy when another person is hurt by saying "I am sorry." The phrase is not a sign of a person's guilt, rather it is seen as a way of showing concern. In addition, duty requires one to physically assist in extricating the injured person from the source of the pain. Among U. S. Americans, especially those of European background, the predominant cultural norm would suggest that a person can display his or her concern through the use of the type of question that Sam had asked. How the question is posed in terms of tone, pitch, and rate indicates the degree of concern. If in fact one is badly hurt, the cultural rule in the United States is that the other person should call for medical help since any attempt to assist physically might exacerbate the pain or injury. There are a few exceptions to this rule, as in the case of administering cardio-pulmonary resuscitation.

In spite of my proficiency in British English, American English was, for the most part, incomprehensible because of differences in pronunciation and use of words. There were numerous instances of miscommunication in which I felt embarrassed because my speech was misunderstood due to the different way in which the words were pronounced or used, or due to my accent. For example, the British pronunciation of the word "schedule" is shedyool; it was pronounced as skedyool by most Americans. Once I used the word "stroke" to explain the punctuation mark in "intrapersonal/ interpersonal communication" in one of my classes. The students were clearly confused by the term because the U. S. American way of saying the phrase would have substituted the word "stroke" with the word "slash." It was another lesson that culture matters. Communication scholars have long argued that the goal of communication is to share meaning. If this is the goal, then the cultural variables that we bring into the context of communication should matter. For in those variables lie the possibilities for understanding or misunderstanding. Throughout the initial period of my American journey, cultural expectations about appropriate conduct and linguistic patterns led to numerous communication failures.

Another equally perplexing issue for me centered around the use of first names to refer to persons in authority or higher in status or age. I could not understand the general informality of my new environment, and I wondered why people would be so disrespectful. Why would fellow classmates, for example, address the instructor by his or her first name? My relationship with authority figures and people older than myself can be explained by what the intercultural scholar Hofstede calls power distance index (PDI).[41] PDI is the degree to which a culture places emphasis or a pecking order (high or low) on such power-relationship issues as age, social status, position, gender, wealth, authority, and so forth. In low PDI cultures, individuals are assumed to be equal and therefore are expected to be treated similarly. In high PDI cultures, individuals are assumed to be unequal and therefore are expected to be treated differentially. For example, people who are older or have higher status because of age, wealth, position, and so on expect to be treated with deference. This deference can be displayed through verbal and nonverbal means such as in greetings styles (handshake, bowing, or kissing on the hand or forehead). To observe most white Americans address the instructor, an authority figure, without such deference was perplexing. At the predominantly African American Howard University, I saw a profound difference in the way black students related to instructors. They referred to them by their formal titles, in contrast to my experience of white students' relationships with instructors at Towson State. At California State University, Sacramento, where I taught, it took me a while to refer to my colleagues by their first names, since doing so in my original culture would be considered a sign of disrespect. In spite of my growth or adjustment in this area, I am still somewhat uncomfortable when students refer to me or other instructors by their first name.

Power distance, the degree to which cultures value equality or inequality among its members, remains a cultural constant in spite of one's level of intercultural growth. A cultural constant is that aspect of one's culture (beliefs, values, norms, and attitudes) that is not so easily amenable to the forces of change, regardless of one's experience in a new environment. How one responds to such differences in distance and one's ability to switch responses from one context to another demonstrates one's level of growth.

The initial period of my American journey also saw other episodes of communication failure. At the college cafeteria and public restaurants, I ordered the same meals all the time for the same reason. On public transportation, I had the habit of paying my fare with large bills as a way of masking my ignorance of the currency. I felt too embarrassed to ask questions since my accent would give me away. To ask any question was to expose myself to vulnerabilities. On a few occasions, I withdrew from the sources of the pain. Many newcomers to the U. S. may experience communication difficulties because the forces that shape and alter human behavior in the United States may be different from the forces that shape the societies they come from. For many, the process of adjustment may take longer.

At no point did it occur to me that the frustrations I experienced on a daily basis were a consequence of the perceptual distance between me and members of the host culture. Nor did it occur to me that the withdrawal from the host environment might be a symptom of the stress associated with adjustment to a new environment or the phenomenon commonly known as culture shock. Our cultures differ because our histories (e.g., wars, slavery), environments (e.g., hot or dry climate), institutions (e.g., religion, government), technologies (e.g., traditional or modern), and communication patterns (e.g., direct or indirect narrative styles) are different. Differences also exist because people are biologically different as in skin color and physical characteristics. The consequence of this lack of awareness is frustration. Yet I believe that with understanding of these differences and acceptance of them, Americans can come to a future when difference no longer makes a difference.

When I left Nigeria, I believed that my life and experiences in the country had fully prepared me for life in another country. Most newcomers to the U. S. believe also that the experiences in their own countries have prepared them for life in the U. S. Nothing can be further from the truth. Upon graduation from college, my parents had encouraged me to accept employment in the western part of Nigeria, an area inhabited by Yorubas, one of the major ethnic groups in the country. My parents, who are Igbos, had lived in western Nigeria and speak the Yoruba language fluently. The Igbos represent one of the three major ethnic groups in the country. My parents also lived for over a quarter of a century in northern Nigeria, where I was born. The north is inhabited largely by Hausas and Fulanis, and my parents also speak the Hausa language fluently.

However, the rise of ethnic antagonisms against the Igbos in the region a few years following Nigeria's independence in 1960 compelled my parents to return to eastern Nigeria, their place of origin. In 1967, eastern Nigeria seceded from the rest of the country to form the Republic of Biafra. Following the collapse of talks to resolve the crisis between the east and the Nigerian government, a bloody civil war ensued. The war, which lasted nearly thirty months, claimed more than one million lives. The period of the Biafra-Nigeria conflict (1967–70) was a very dark chapter in the country's history, and many accounts of that ugly experience have been written. Thus just as the history of slavery has shaped black-white relations in the U. S., the history of the Nigeria-Biafra war has shaped inter-ethnic relations in Nigeria. Communication in such areas as politics, education, the military, the economy, and infrastructural development has always been tainted by the above historical circumstances, yet it was difficult for me to recognize the profound impact of history on race relations in the U. S. I will return to this point later.

Developing an Identity

Although I was born in the northern region of Nigeria, I cannot claim it as my origin. According to Igbo custom, one's father's place of birth is the person's place of origin. In other words, my father's place of birth in the eastern region is my place of origin. In the same manner, my father's place of origin is his father's place of birth. Consider for example the following: if my father was born in California and I was born in Arkansas, California, according to my culture, would constitute my place of origin. On the other hand, if my grandfather was born in California, and my father was born in New York and I was born in Arkansas, both my father and I would hail from my grandfather's birthplace. Africans, Asians, Latinos, and persons from mostly non-Western cultures generally maintain their family lines and group identity from one generation to the next through this means. In the U. S., a person's place of birth is his or her place of origin. Thus if one is born in California, the state would constitute the person's place of origin regardless of whether the father was born in California, Arkansas, or New York. This difference, also, may account for why Americans (especially of European ancestry) feel no link to their great-grandparents' role before the civil war. Most do not know it. For many, the question "Are you Irish, English, or German?" is relevant only on St. Patrick's Day or during Oktoberfest and the like, or as an excuse to travel. I had initial difficulty and disconnectedness, like most newcomers to the U. S., in conversations with U. S. Americans in comprehending how this sense of looseness would engender group identity and a collective spirit among the different groups in the society.

My worldview, a combination of my beliefs and values, collided with fundamental teachings about what is logical and illogical in the context of cultural patterns and communication styles in Western society. For example, while old age in African society is highly valued, most U. S. Americans place a high value on youth. Furthermore, the value placed on communal/group responsibility for rearing a child (it takes a village to raise a child) contrasts heavily with the Western notion of individualism (only the parents can raise the child). In addition, the value placed on the extended family system contrasts greatly with the value placed on the nuclear family in the United States. The underlying principle in Igbo society is "I am because we are, and since we are therefore I am." This differs markedly from the Western view of individualism as reflected in the work of René Descartes, the seventeenth-century French philosopher who noted, *cogito ergo sum* (meaning "I think, therefore I am"). In African culture, one does not exist in isolation from the group. Thus the concept of individualism is very hard to comprehend, especially by a new immigrant from a communal-based culture.

An equally puzzling issue for me was the reaction of most U. S. Americans to my family background. I come from a fairly large extended family with some history of polygyny. Polygyny is the union between a man and two or more wives, whereas polygamy refers to marriage among several spouses, for example a woman who marries more than one husband or a man who marries more than one wife. Polygyny is an accepted and respected marriage form in traditional Igbo society. My father, Chief Clement Muoghalu Nwosu, had two wives. My paternal grandfather, Chief Ezekwesili Nwosu, was married to four. My great-grandfather, Chief Odoji, also married to four wives, was the chief priest and custodian of traditional religion in my town. I come from Umudioka town, a small rural community in Anambra State of the Federal Republic of Nigeria.

My maternal grandfather from the royal line of the Akaigwe clan, Chief Nwokoye Akaigwe, was the traditional ruler of Enugwu-Ukwu, a medium-sized community in Anambra State. Chief Akaigwe was known for several firsts. He was the first warrant chief[42] in Enugwu-Ukwu, the first to own and ride a bicycle, the first to own a car, the first to build a "zinc" house (metal roofing as opposed to thatched roof in Enugu-Ukwu). He was married to twenty-four women. I found myself explaining (to the curiosity, and sometimes amazement, of my U. S. friends) that the traditional economic structure in Igbo society dictated this familial arrangement whereby a man would marry more than one spouse and produce several children, who then assist him with farm work, regarded as the fiber and glue of economic life in traditional Igbo society. Each spouse and her own children live in a separate home built by the husband. Each wife is responsible for the up-keep of her immediate family with support from the husband.

One of the traditions of my extended family is the family reunion held every two years. Families unable to attend for any reason are required to send in their pictures so that other members of the extended family present at the reunion may know them. The goal of the family reunion is to encourage unity, promote awareness of each other, and prevent the potential for incest or marital union between and among family relatives, considered an abomination in Igboland.

In traditional Igbo society, it is acceptable for a man to marry many women to support the economic wellbeing of the family. Coming from an agrarian society where peoples' livelihood depended on subsistence farming, it made sense to understand the institution of polygyny as a fundamental pillar of traditional Igbo economy and society. Today, however, a person may marry more than one wife with the approval of the first wife, mostly in instances where the first wife fails to conceive a male child, a requirement for perpetuating the family and ancestral lineage. (Missing from this view, of course, is a biological understanding of conception.)

While the extended family system exists in the United States, the degree to which it is important varies, in contrast to African culture. During the initial period of my journey, it was clear that the nuclear family was the norm, although other kinds of families (e.g., single-parent families) have emerged. Former vice president Al Gore captures this change well in his book Joined at the Heart: The Transformation of the American Family. I was surprised to learn that most U. S. families did not worry about whether the child was male or female. This is certainly not the case in Africa.

A related issue centered around my perception of matrimonial life in my culture compared with U.S. society. For example, among the Igbos, marriage, in the context of the extended family system, does not only bring together husband and wife in matrimonial life, but it also unites the couple's two families in a stronger relationship. When a person marries in Igboland, he/she does not establish an independent family. The couple enters into an already existing family. The idea of exclusively mutual love between spouses that I saw in the U. S. was an aberration. In the Igbo culture, marital love is multidimensional. One enters into love not only with his/her spouse, but with all members of the family (i.e., both families). Marriage for the Igbo people is not a pact between two individuals—man and woman. Marriage for the Igbos is a community affair, a pact between two umunnas (extended families). This is the case in most non-Western cultures, and for most newcomers to the U. S. As we know, a majority of these newcomers come from places other than Europe.

The differing perceptions about the institution of marriage and the extended family system presented initial challenges for me. We know that institutional arrangements relate to how a society organizes itself through formal structures. Such things as the form of government, the educational system, religious institutions, and marriage and family structures constitute a society's institutional set-up. Within this set-up then is the question of role differentiation, i.e., how people relate to one another. In the U. S., for most people of European background, the core of social life revolves around commitment to self and personal freedom. As an African, it is always difficult for me to draw the line between this commitment to self and personal freedom and the commitment to interdependence and community. The non-individuality of the African, a vital part of the African cultural ethos, provided a basis for the numerous misperceptions and misinterpretations on my part of U. S. cultural values.

History and Communication

Among many Americans, an often overlooked but critical element of communication is the extent to which historical forces shape human interaction processes in the United States. Indeed, obstacles to competent communication activities among U. S. Americans, and between old and new immigrants, can be bridged merely through an understanding of the powerful influence of historical forces on human behavior. These forces include slavery, conflict, war, colonialism, famine, and prosperity. These forces represent the collective wisdom of a group. To deny or ignore that history is to deny the experience of the group to which that particular history makes sense. To deny the Holocaust experience, for example, is to deny the experience of the Jewish people—the Holocaust is a major historical force which has shaped how Jews have come to view the world around them. To deny the internment experience for the Japanese is to deny their suffering in the U. S. during World War II. To deny the massive displacement and expropriation of Native American Indians, including the deaths of many when they were moved from their lands to Oklahoma (in what has come to be known as the Trail of Tears), is to minimize a horrific historical experience that has had a profound impact on the lives of Native American Indians in the U. S. To deny the experience of the Irish in the 1840s in Boston with regard to discrimination is to deny a major historical force which shaped Irish life in this country. Finally, one cannot ignore the history of the women's suffrage movement, one of the most dramatic political battles fought in the U. S. from 1840 through 1920 to extend freedom and equality to American women, a struggle for equality that continues today.

In the same manner, to deny or ignore the experience of slavery for American blacks is to deny or ignore a major historical force which has shaped and continues to shape the collective wisdom of African Americans in this country. There is no question that people bring their histories to a communication event. When African Americans react negatively to Ross Perot's choice of words, as in "you people" during an address to them in Texas during the 1992 U. S. presidential campaign, the reaction draws from the experience of slavery where a "master-servant" relationship existed between blacks and whites. The term "you people" may not imply a put down, and Ross Perot may not have intend to put down his Texas audience. However, the language "you people" does tend to separate and could lead to misperceptions and a communication breakdown. Placed in the historical context of slavery, such language use is a reminder to American blacks that they are lower in status than whites. Clearly history matters and it shapes a group's culture. In our discourse on race relations, we must be mindful of history, as individuals bring this to their interaction processes. Newcomers bring their histories with them to the U. S.

Some of my initial culture bumps in the U. S. emerged from a lack of understanding of some of the forces of history which have shaped domestic relations in this country, and of their implications for competent communication in a variety of contexts. At Howard University, I used the term "old boy"[43] in referring to an African American classmate during a conversation. While this is a positive term used when addressing one's friends in Nigeria, my African American friend took offense at what appeared to suggest a master-servant relationship between him and myself, because during the period of slavery, African American men were referred to as "boy" by their white masters, implying less than full manhood. Through discussion, we were able to recognize that no offense was intended, and we both grew from the experience.

Allowing Room for Mistakes

A gap in black-white interactions in particular, and race relations in general, in America today is the inability to allow room for mistakes. If America is to move beyond race, we must also be willing to engage in genuine dialogue that helps to sort out the cultural differences that create the culture bumps and the miscommunication in the first place. Through such dialogue of engagement, intercultural understanding is enhanced. Without such dialogue, people who come from differing cultural backgrounds are likely to shut off communication or feel that they must walk on eggshells when attempting to communicate. Such a feeling chills the atmosphere for positive human interactions and the potential for building strong communities.

Overall, growth for me throughout my American journey has produced greater functional adaptability such that I am now able to experience cultural differences with better understanding and at the same time to function well today as an American citizen. Although my expectations are still grounded in Igbo cultural values, they have been shaped through frequent travels and interactions with other U. S. citizens in both small communities and large cities across the country. I have visited over thirty-five states since my arrival in this country. I have traveled to large urban cities such as Washington, D.C., New Orleans, New York, Chicago, Los Angeles, San Francisco, Miami, and Atlanta; to mid-sized towns such as Sacramento, Portland, Nashville, East Lansing, and Albuquerque; and to small rural communities such as Oakdale, LA, Myrtle Beach, SC, and Arcata, CA (where the city council passed the first ordinance against the Patriot Act, challenging its intrusion on civil liberties). I have spent time in Plains, GA, hometown of President Jimmy Carter. I have participated and immersed myself in the varied historical, institutional, and community events that cut across racial, ethnic, and cultural boundaries. Among them are religious services of other faiths, Hispanic Cinco De Mayo, African American Juneteenth Day, a Native American Indian pow-wow, German Oktoberfest, Chinese New Year, an East Indian wedding, Thanksgiving dinner, and several more.

Through prolonged and varied intercultural communication experiences, newcomers to the U. S. can gradually acquire the communication skills necessary for coping with the challenges of diversity and life in the U. S., and at the same time realize America's immense promise. They must be part of, and not apart from, the multicultural American experience. They must engage in actions that move them further in this direction. This interaction is essential to building an inclusive American community.

❧ ⑤ ❧

BLACK-LATINO RELATIONS

Whenever there's any population shift, there's always a fear that the new people are going to throw out the old.

Anonymous California state legislator

Blacks, who feel they waited longest and endured most in the fight for equal opportunity, are uneasy about being supplanted by Hispanics or, in some areas, by Asians as the numerically largest and most influential minority—and even more, about being outstripped in wealth and status by these newer groups. Because Hispanics are so numerous and Asians such a fast-growing group, they have become the "hot" minorities, and blacks feel their needs are getting lower priority.

William A. Henry III

There is the fable of the big white dog sitting on a porch with a large loaf of bread, and a bunch of black, brown, and yellow dogs yapping outside the fence, coveting the bread. Whenever the colored dogs got close enough to the fence to annoy the big white dog, he'd pull off a morsel of bread, hardly more than a crumb, and throw it out to the howling hordes. Then, enjoying his own bread, he'd sit back and watch the other dogs fight over crumbs. There may be some lessons in this fable for Black and Brown folks as the Latino population grows.

Julianne Malveaux

What Latinos have learned is what their counterparts learned in the city of Lynwood—wait, increase the voter rolls, and when they reach critical mass, seize the power.

Nicolas Vaca

Black-Latino Relations

More than fifteen years ago, in a 1990 issue of Time magazine, William Henry III, a staff writer for Time, commented about the uneasiness among American blacks regarding the rising Latino population in the U. S.[44] Black uneasiness, according to Henry, stemmed from three factors: first, blacks believe they have waited the longest and endured the most in the fight for equality and justice and the presence of Latinos weakens their prospects for more black access to resources in a nation that has not treated them fairly; second, blacks fear being supplanted by Latinos as the nation's most influential minority group; and third, blacks fear being outstripped in wealth and consequently in status by, in their view, this new group to America.

The last few years have witnessed a significant rise in the Latino population, thus making them the nation's largest and fastest growing minority population, exacerbating black fears as identified above, and consequently increasing the tension in black-Latino relations. Indeed, if ever there was any doubt about the fragile and competitive nature of black-Latino relations, it can be seen in the racial skirmishes between students from both groups in our nation's public schools, in the shifting alliances among both groups in the direction of where there is the largest gain for each group, and in voting booths across the nation.

The 2001 mayoral election in Los Angeles for example revealed, to some degree, the nature of the fragile and competitive relationship between both groups. The election—a contest between the former Speaker of the California State Assembly Antonio Villaraigosa, a Latino, and white city attorney James Hahn, both Democrats, ended in defeat for the once-powerful speaker. Villaraigosa lost to an unusual amalgam of whites and blacks. In fact, 80 percent of the black vote went to Hahn, who also won 59 percent of the white vote. Villaraigosa secured 82 percent of the Latino vote, and as much as 54 percent of the Jewish vote, not enough to install him as the first Latino mayor of Los Angeles in over a century.

In 2005, Villaraigosa ran again, this time, with support from the black community. He defeated Hahn in a run-off election to become the first Latino to govern Angelinos in more than one hundred years. Villaraigosa won nearly 60 percent of the black votes, a huge contrast to the less than 20 percent of the black electorate that voted for him fours years earlier.

Political scientist Raphael Sonenshein has noted that the really interesting question is "what happens to relations between Latinos and blacks now."[45] Sonenshein's question is worth exploring in full because black support for a Latino candidate is by no means, in his words, "the sign of a full-scale coalition."[46]

What accounts for the growing pains in black-Latino relations? And what must African Americans and Latinos do to bridge the gap? To understand this emerging divide, we must first examine the history of both the African American and Latino experiences in the U. S. Second, we must examine the differing perceptions in both communities about themselves and about each other brought about, in part, by their differing historical experiences. Third, we must explore some consequences for both groups of a strain in black-Latino relations, and finally, we must chart a course for moving beyond the politics and the narrow vision of ethnicity that threatens to widen the chasm between these ethnic groups.

Black-Latino Relations; Two Histories

Any attempt to understand the growing tension in black-Latino relations must begin first with a discussion of the historical experiences of both groups in the U. S. Much is known about the African American experience in the U. S. Much has been written about slavery and the quest for free labor as the driving engine behind the black presence in America. Nearly four hundred years since the first set of Africans arrived on the shores of Jamestown, Virginia, much continues to be written about the institution of slavery and state-church complicity in the denial of basic rights that officially defined the nature of black-white relations in America. Even today, nearly two hundred years after slavery was abolished, and just about forty years after the historic Civil Rights Act of 1964, the black struggle for freedom remains fundamental to the existence of black America.

However, because American blacks have been consumed by their long personal and collective struggles for freedom, few have paid attention to the historical struggle for those same rights reflected in the Latino experience in America. Moreover, the paucity of research on the Hispanic experience in the U. S. further complicates any knowledge or understanding regarding the Latino freedom struggle. Most Americans, including blacks, tend to associate

Latino history with immigration, and believe that most Spanish speakers are immigrants. This is not the case. Most Americans, including blacks, in fact are unaware that Americans of Hispanic heritage have a varied history and a complicated ancestry that dates back more than four hundred years. Americans of Hispanic origin are from birth "the result of the encounter of diverse people such as the Spaniards and the Portuguese with the diverse Indian nations of America such as the Incas, Aztecs, Quechuas, Mayas, Tainos, Siboneyes and others."[47] Americans of Hispanic origin are also the result of encounters with African peoples who were brought by force as slaves to the Americas. From these encounters emerged the different Latino people of Peru, Bolivia, Colombia, El Salvador, Mexico, Cuba, Puerto Rico, Dominican Republic, Brazil, and other Latin American countries.[48]

Indeed, contrary to popular opinion, "there are Spanish-speaking Californians, New Mexicans, or Texans whose ancestors lived in the Southwest long before their respective states became part of the United States."[49] In their authoritative account entitled The Hispanics in the United States: A History, Stanford University scholars L. H. Gann and Peter Duignan note that Hispanics, like the vast majority of other Americans, trace their original homes to different countries including Mexico, Puerto Rico, Cuba, Nicaragua, El Salvador, Honduras, Spain, and Argentina. "Some of them are proficient in Spanish, although others have lost the use of their ancestral tongue. Some are indifferent to their cultural inheritance and regard themselves as un-hyphenated Americans: others have a strong commitment to their Hispanic legacy. Some are rich and some are poor; some are conservative and some are radical; some are fair-skinned and some are swarthy or black."[50]

The U. S. annexed approximately 50 percent of Mexico's territory, along with its inhabitants, in 1848, forming what is now referred to as the Southwest.[51] These lands had been Spanish and then Mexican territories for more than three hundred years before becoming U. S. lands. The indigenous peoples and cultures, the Hispanic culture, and the new mestizo or Latino culture thus became an integral part of the U. S. and American culture.

Latinos and Slavery

What is also significant in the context of black-Latino relations is that few blacks recognize the historic opposition to slavery by Latinos in the 1800s. Emerging historical accounts suggest that it was the opposition to American engagement in slavery that aroused a bitter debate in the U. S. over war with Mexico. L. H. Gann and Peter Duignan write that those who were the principal advocates of war with Mexico were southerners who wanted to safeguard slavery as an institution within the U. S. through the creation of a new or even several new slave states. This desire became the imperative that shaped the discourse between those who were for war and those against war. The anti-war movement, already opposed to slavery, believed that the annexation of Texas was a conspiracy led by slave owners to essentially undermine American freedom and basic human rights. Given the charged atmosphere, James Polk, U. S. president at the time, decided on what seemed to be a middle-course solution to "satisfy both the slave states and the 'free soil' states: he would acquire not only Texas but also Oregon and California, thus extending America's boundaries to the Pacific ocean." [52] President Polk not only made good on his quest by acquiring Texas and California, but he also acquired New Mexico, and purchased Oregon from the British. Indeed all of the Western/Southwestern states of the U. S.— California, New Mexico, Arizona, Nevada, Utah, Colorado, Wyoming, and Texas—were all Mexican territories until 1848 when the Mexican-American war ended.

The Story of Texas

The story of Texas is particularly important because the immediate cause for the Mexican-American war that began in 1846 derived from disputes over the territory and what behaviors were permissible within it. As English and German settlers from the U. S. flooded the province to engage in plantation agriculture with the aid of slave labor, the Mexican government began to insist that the newcomers abide by Mexican laws. One such law outlawed slavery. The position of the Mexican government incensed the newcomers, most of them from the American South, who argued that Mexican laws undermined their inalienable rights and their professed notion of "manifest destiny." In 1836 the newcomers, taking advantage of the weaknesses in the Mexican leadership, declared Texas an independent sovereign state. The Mexican government under President Antonio López de Santa Anna tried to crush the rebellion, but failed due to the political problems it was facing at home.

The next ten years saw strong political debates in the U. S. on whether the country should go to war to acquire Texas and the rich territories of California and New Mexico, also at the time belonging to Mexico. The British, who were no friends of the Americans at the time, also had interests in these territories. While Mexico was willing to let Texas remain an independent sovereign state and was being pressured by the British to recognize it as such, the Mexican government feared that the annexation of Texas by the U. S. might lead to the loss of other Mexican territories. The U. S., on its own, feared that any failure to act might give advantage over these vast territories and the Pacific to the British, who already had a controlling presence in Australia and New Zealand. In 1846, following months of wrangling, finger pointing, and counter-accusations, Mexico and the U. S. went to war, with the U. S. defeating the Mexican army, forcing Mexico to sign a peace treaty with the Americans on February 2, 1848. The treaty, signed at Guadalupe Hidalgo near Mexico City, surrendered control of California and New Mexico to the U. S.

Although Mexico lost the war, the Treaty of Guadalupe Hidalgo provided guarantees that while these territories no longer belonged to Mexico, the U. S. government would respect the property, religious, and cultural rights (including language rights) of citizens of the conquered territories. In fact, as part of the treaty and to prevent any future claims, the U. S. government paid Mexico $15 million in cash in exchange for the territories, and another $3.25 million for claims made by American citizens on the Mexican government as a result of the war.

The propensity to expand the American frontier through the acquisition of land held by Latinos (especially Mexico) in the heyday of the American experiment has been a defining fissure in Latino-white relations. Each conquered territory resulted in the subjugation of Latinos into second-class citizens. The Hispanic struggles for justice have therefore been with respect to these rights, and the Treaty of Guadalupe Hidalgo provides the basis for those struggles, and thus is seen by many Latinos as the most important document for American Hispanics.

The Latino Population

While the Latino population in the U. S. has been around for more than five hundred years, the rapid growth in its population began in the late1960s as a result of refugee movements, immigration reform, and illegal immigration from several Latin American countries. By 1970, the U. S. government coined the term "Hispanic" to refer to people who were born in any of the Spanish-speaking countries of the Americas or people who could trace their ancestry to Spain or former colonial territories of Spain. However, few Latinos refer to themselves as Hispanics.

By 1980, Americans witnessed large Latino migrant populations settling in such places as New York, Trenton, Newark, Buffalo, and Providence in the Northeast; Miami, Houston, Atlanta, and Washington, D. C in the South; Las Vegas, Sacramento, San Jose, Santa Rosa, Anaheim, San Diego, and Los Angeles in the West; and Chicago and Lake County, Illinois, in the Midwest. In the last two decades, in some of the areas mentioned, ethnic Latino enclaves have emerged, while in others, Latinos have assimilated fully in multi-ethnic neighborhoods.

The latest Census Bureau numbers show that across the country, Latinos are now the nation's largest minority group, numbering about 37 million, compared with approximately 36.2 million blacks. These numbers represent a 4.7 percent rise in the Latino population since April 2000, compared with a 1.5 percent rise in the black population, and 0.8 percent increase for Americans of European background, whose population currently stands at 196 million. The current surge in the Latino population is due essentially to higher birth rates and a huge wave of immigration, including illegal immigration. By the end of the 1990s, about 50 percent of new immigrants who came to the U. S. came from Latin America, compared to 1970 when only 19 percent of new immigrants came from the region.[53] Given current trends, demographers project that by 2050, the U. S. population will be 47 percent European American, 29 percent Latino, 13 percent African American, 9 percent Asian American, and 1.0 percent Native American Indian. And about 19 percent of the nation's population at that time will be immigrant.[54] These numbers are important in assessing how each group jockeys for a fair share of the national cake.

Different Experiences, Different Perceptions

The differing historical experiences of American blacks and American Hispanics provide an important framework for examining the differing perceptions of each other in both communities. But any such examination must draw from three explanations: a psychological explanation, a cultural explanation, and a political explanation. The psychological explanation is crucial because it provides a prism to understanding the how and why of the fragile nature of black-Latino relations in America. The cultural explanation offers a window for understanding the nature and consequences of the culture gap between the two ethnic minorities, and the political explanation provides a framework for exploring the basis for the emerging political divide between Hispanic America and black America.

A Psychological Explanation

Communication scholars, whose discipline has been informed a great deal by psychology, make the case that human interactions are motivated by certain needs and desires. When people affiliate with others, they do so because such affiliation satisfies a particular need. It seems to me that black-Latino relations can be likened to the sort of relations developed by two battered women who experience a low point in their lives because of abuse from their spouses or friends. The parallel experience of both women, an experience grounded in victimization, is precisely the basis or the reason for the functional relationship. Thus they become friends only because they have something in common. They see themselves as victims. They perform the mutually satisfying function of comforting each other. But once they get past the psychological feeling of pain and helplessness, they see no more need for the function.

It seems to me that one of the major crises of meaning in black-Latino relations in America lies in this type of functional relationship. Black America and Hispanic America see each other as victims of an oppressive regime. The common enemy is white. They come together to share a common feeling or attitude toward a perceived enemy, in this case, a negative attitude. Once the attitude is gone, the temporary friendship is gone. The friendship after all is based on the psychological need to find succor in others who share common problems. Without appearing simplistic, what binds the two groups together is the common enemy, nothing substantive, and nothing tangible. Here is a typical conversation overheard between two angry members of both ethnic groups over their failure to secure admission into a university graduate program:

> Black male: Man, I can't believe they wouldn't let me into the program.
>
> Latino male: Me too, that sucks.
>
> Black male: That department is so racist.
>
> Latino male: I was so qualified. I have been trying to get in since last year. And I hear there are no Mexicans in that program.
>
> Black male: You know, that's right, you're right, I never thought about that.
>
> Latino male: I'm tired of being put down by white people. Those racists!
>
> Black male: Yeah, me too. I have had enough of being put down.

As you might guess, these two men both walked out together bonded by their common experience—a shared history of victimization, so to speak—without knowing anything about each other. What brings them together is that they are victims, and the relationship ends there, at the contact stage. The tragedy in the type of dialogue reflected by the two men is that the reliance on a common set of negative feelings towards a problem does nothing to enhance the relationship between the individuals. If black-Latino relations are to improve, the relations must move beyond this type of casual contact. What is needed is a new kind of involvement and social bonding between both groups, where a sense of mutuality of being connected is present, and both groups learn more about each other, and make a commitment to further each other's purpose. Real friendships and alliances begin with the desire to build lasting and sustained friendships.

A Cultural Explanation

Real friendships do not grow and flourish in an environment where participants do not know one another. Given my knowledge of both communities, I believe that the cultural explanation for the differing perceptions between American blacks and Latinos draws fundamentally from this problem. Indeed, a culture gap does exist between Hispanic America and black America. Both ethnic groups understand little of each other. The negative cultural stereotypes and the subterranean current of animosity between the groups further exemplify this gap. In truth, most Latinos are aware of the black experience, but few understand black culture. The distinction between the black experience and black culture is important here, because the former reflects the African American experience with slavery and its legacy of racism (of which most Latinos are aware), while the latter speaks to African American cultural patterns and communication style (which few Latinos understand).

Few Latinos recognize that the majority of blacks who came to the U. S. brought with them a strong cultural heritage, which later became grounded in the spirituality of the Baptist faith. Under the weight of European oppression and exploitation, however, American blacks lost a great deal of their true cultural and ethnic identities. Thus Alex Haley's compelling book Roots, and its subsequent adaptation as a national television series, provided a spiritual lift in the cultural psyche of American blacks. Roots also transformed blacks in terms of their self-esteem and spurred a new movement that placed Africa at the center of the cultural lives of African Americans.

While accounts of Africanisms or African cultural retentions in America have been provided in the numerous volumes on African history stored in various libraries across America, it is clear that not one major African language of the more than two hundred and fifty languages spoken by blacks brought in chains to the Americas survived. What we know today as black language in America is a patchwork of West African languages and English that most linguists and scholars now refer to as Ebonics. Ebonics has its own structure, syntax, and pragmatics, and various dialects of the language are spoken by black people in many parts of the U. S., especially in the South. A much more original strand of this language is used by the black people of Gullah who inhabit parts of Georgia, South Carolina, Florida, and the Sea Islands off the coast of Florida. Although Ebonics is looked down upon as incorrect English, it is not. Most educated and middle-class blacks clearly identify with it. They find great comfort and pleasure in the use of this language and have developed the capacity to alternate between their native tongue and Standard American English. Factors that govern a person's desire to switch linguistic codes are the subject of the conversation, the context of the conversation, and the gender of conversational partners. While Spanish is the lingua franca of many Latinos in the U. S., a new language, Spanglish—a patchwork of Spanish and English—is emerging as the third most important language for Latinos. Like most blacks, many Latinos are also able to alternative between these languages depending on the subject, the context, and the gender of conversational partners. But as Richard Rodriguez notes, Español (or Spanish) is "my family's language."

A family member would say something to me (in Español) and I would feel myself specially recognized. My parents would say something to me and I would feel embraced by the sounds of their words. Those sounds said: I am speaking with ease in Spanish. I am addressing you in words I never use with los gringos (Europeans). I recognize you as someone special, close, like no one outside. You belong to us. In the family.[55]

In a sense, the use of these languages in black and Hispanic America suggests a particular comfort level and a strong feeling of belonging that one does not necessarily have when one uses a language outside of one's cultural experience. Language is an important instrument for maintaining group identity.

Black cultural patterns and communication styles are also a patchwork of Africanisms and some (not all) European American ways. The European ways present in African American cultural patterns and communication styles reflect the historical experience of American blacks in the context of slavery. For example, inherent in Ebonics is a communication style that values animation, is loud, colorful, overt, and very straightforward. This approach to communication, which draws from both African (animated, loud, and colorful) and European (direct, overt, and straightforward) ways, flies in the face of what is considered appropriate communication style among Hispanics. In comparison to American blacks, Latino communication style is less animated, less direct, and has a much greater focus on face-saving. Since few Latinos understand black communication style, most of them generally perceive blacks as rude and disrespectful.

A similar cultural ignorance about Latinos is equally present in black America, where many blacks are not only unaware of the Latino struggle for justice in America, but more importantly do not understand Latino cultural patterns and communication styles. Latinos, for example, place a great deal of emphasis on respect for the elderly, and this respect is reflected in how language is used. There is also a relationship between one's status or hierarchy and the level of respect one receives from subordinates. Furthermore, there is a strong religious faith in Latino culture shaped by a Catholic tradition. The common phrase, "Uno nunca se olvida de Dios," or "One should never forget about God," guides how one relates to self and to others. The loud, outspoken person, and the one who talks about his or her accomplishments and how good the individual looks, is looked down upon in Latino culture. Modesty then is the soul of communication in Latino culture. Few blacks recognize and understand this fundamental cultural pattern and communication style of Latinos, and sometimes view Latinos as too cagey to be trusted.

Under the present dispensation, ethnic misconceptions and negative stereotypes about each group have found expression and welcome in candid conversations in both communities. Anti-black and anti-Latino sentiments and prejudices, including the use of racial slurs, now abound on both sides of the ethnic divide. It is not uncommon in the Latino community (especially in California) to hear such racial slurs as mayate (the Spanish equivalent of the word nigger) hurled around in reference to the black community. The 2001 loss of the mayoral elections in Los Angeles reflects the increasing level of distrust in both communities. As one African American legislator who was berated for supporting Speaker Villaraigosa told the Los Angeles Times, "I got heat from blacks. They asked, 'Why do you support him? He'll throw us all out.'"[56] Although this has not happened since Villaraigosa became mayor following the 2005 mayoral elections, why would many blacks believe, in the first place, that he would throw them out if he became the city's mayor? What is the source of this fear? At the hub of the growing pain in black-Latino relations is the political explanation.

A Political Explanation

In the last two decades, blacks have perceived the tremendous growth in Latino population as a threat to black political power. This may explain why many blacks voted against Villaraigosa. Even more startling was black opposition to unchecked or unregulated immigration when many blacks in California voted for the famous Proposition 187. Exit polls showed that 56 percent of African Americans and 64 percent of whites voted in favor of Proposition 187. According to exit polls, about 31 percent of Latinos, also voted, surprisingly, for the proposition. Proposition 187 barred illegal immigrants from receiving public support throughout California's public education system, and required public educational institutions to verify the legal status of both immigrant students and their parents. Proposition 187 also required all providers of publicly-funded, non-emergency health care services to verify the legal status of persons seeking services in order to be reimbursed by the state. In addition, Proposition 187 made the production and use of false documents a state felony, and required all service providers to report suspected illegal immigrants to law enforcement authorities and to the Immigration and Naturalization Service (INS), now the Bureau of U. S. Citizenship and Immigration Services.

Proposition 187 was based on the simple premise that denying public services to illegal immigrants would discourage them from coming to the U. S. We know that most of the illegal immigrants to California who would be affected by Proposition 187 were Latinos. Most came from Mexico, and many of them worked as migrants on farms and in garment shops. Many blacks ironically voted for Proposition 187 not so much because they were, in principle, supportive of the issues of the proposition (that illegal immigrants were draining state resources needed for other areas of governance), but merely because of anti-Latino feelings on what was perceived as the emerging threat to black political strength posed by a growing Latino population in California. The feelings are the same in several southern and midwestern states where there is a growing Latino population. Thus the politics of numbers have outweighed any serious effort at controlling or managing the complexities of illegal immigration in the country.

As we have seen since the passage of Proposition 187 in California, denying public services to illegal or undocumented immigrants has not been an easy task. Many public agencies have refused to comply with its verification requirements, fearing that Proposition 187 affects innocent people. How does one, for example, deal with the U. S.-born child, children, or family members, all U. S. citizens by law, of a so-called illegal immigrant now living in the U. S.? While Proposition 187 was presented as an honest attempt to address a serious federal problem, the motivations became muddied in accusations that the proposition was racially or ethnically tainted.

There is a deep-seated feeling in black America today that Hispanics (and other groups) have benefited too much from the spoils of the freedom struggle without making any substantive contribution to the struggle. While blacks have fought hard, more than any other group in America, for affirmative action, public housing, and desegregation in public schools, they worry that groups whose history and experience do not compare to the black experience are now benefiting at the same level from the gains won in these areas. Any growth in Latino population is therefore viewed in the context of what it means for the black share of the national cake.

Syndicated columnist Julianne Malveaux, an African American, captured this feeling well in a series of questions she posed in her analysis of the election of Assemblyman Cruz Bustamante as lieutenant governor of California, the first Latino to hold this position in more than a hundred years. "What happens," Malveaux asked "when demographic shifts suggest that gains African Americans fought hard for must now be shared? Are we interested in offering the same affirmative action for which we have long fought? Or will we emulate Whites in forcing our Latino brothers and sisters to wrest gains from us."[57] There is an undercurrent of feeling in black America that these gains cannot be shared. There is also a perception in black America that Latinos think that they are next to white because of their fair skin. Related to this perception is the politics of race in America, which have historically (rightly or wrongly) classified Latinos as white because of their skin color. The consequence of this is the emergence of the feeling in black America that Latinos' light skin has provided certain white-skin privileges to American Hispanics that have been denied to blacks. But this argument is illogical because it ignores the fact that light-skinned blacks have also benefited from certain white-skin privileges, and they have not been denied access to the gains of the freedom struggle.

The root of some of the anti-black sentiments in the Latino community can be found in this sad state of affairs. Writes Malveaux, "I'll never forget sitting on a panel with a Latino brother who excoriated African American leadership for taking all of the political spoils and leaving 'crumbs' for Latinos. Strident and angry, the man went down a list of our best and brightest, pronouncing them all insensitive and corrupt. 'Wait until we get our turn,' he spat."[58]

Common Problems, Common Ownership

Black America and Hispanic America cannot afford to wait until each gets its turn to hurt the other. Black and Latino historical struggles for freedom and justice are so intertwined that separation and divorce cannot be the most genuine pathway for progress in America and for building an American community. First, both groups must transcend the narrow vision about their common historical struggle. The vision of a common feeling about "the enemy," without anything substantive for sustained and lasting friendship, must end. Second, both communities must begin to build a culture of respect for each other. Building a culture of respect begins with closing the culture gap between both groups, and removing long-standing negative cultural stereotypes that have become the perceptual lens through which each community has filtered the other for years. Third, genuine cooperation and partnership must guide black-Latino relations.

In point of fact, there have been a few examples in which both groups have come together over common problems. In 1988, for example, when César Chávez, the charismatic labor leader, went on a thirty-six-day fast to fight for migrant farm workers' rights, the Reverend Jesse Jackson and several activists came on board to participate. But the struggles for justice in both communities are often narrowly perceived in ethnic terms, rather than in terms of a broad-based coalition for change. The sentiment present but often not expressed is that "It's not really my problem, I'm only here to help you." In this context, farm workers' struggle for justice is seen solely as a Latino struggle. The struggle for civil rights is seen solely as a black struggle. Sadly, when blacks or Latinos or other groups become involved in these causes, they do so because they simply want to help. There is not a feeling of ownership in the involvement.

The fact of the matter is that the struggle for farm worker's rights is not just a Latino struggle, and civil rights ought not to be seen as a black struggle either. The origins of the struggles are certainly ethnic. But ethnic claims to ownership for these causes do serious damage to the struggles for justice. These struggles are purely struggles for human rights. We must cease to view them with ethnic lenses. And we must expand the freedom movement to include other groups and build broader coalitions for these causes. We are a weaker nation when any group is kept down.

Requiem for Civil Rights

Now we hear voices in America arguing that Dr. King's struggle is over—that we've reached the promised land. Maybe they're just carried away by the arrival of the Millennium, and are deluding themselves that when the calender turns to the year 2000, human beings will have been perfected.

Al Gore

I almost weep when I see what has happened to the civil rights movement, the bloody struggles for racial justice … So much that was won over the bites of police dogs, the truncheons of bigoted cops, has been diluted—or lost.

Carl T. Rowan

The masses of our people recognize that most of the defining issues of the Civil Rights Movement no longer exist. We face an unprecedented crisis of poverty, violence, joblessness, and social despair, and the old approaches are no longer sufficient or viable.

Manning Marable

We should not lose our sense of how the civil rights movement happened … In blurring, or ignoring, the context of the struggle, the veneration of Martin Luther King becomes devoid of depth and context, and the ability to use his model to renew the struggle for a just and equitable society is lost.

Andrew Young

Requiem for Civil Rights

If the harsh truth has to be told, it is that the civil rights movement in America is dead. It died following the death of Dr. Martin Luther King, Jr. It died following the decimation of the Black Panthers. Today's civil rights leaders are leaders in name, not in deed. They lack vision. They lack commitment. They lack focus. And they lack praxis. It is time for them to close shop or to regroup.

For more than a quarter of a century, they have watched helplessly as America's right has mounted successful frontal attacks on the gains won by King and the civil rights community. It has been an attack on affirmative action. Now, the attack is on voting rights. And who knows what will be next. For America, it has been one step forward, two steps backward. And the nation's courts have become willing partners in the funeral march for civil rights. If America is to move beyond race, it must provide genuine guarantees for civil liberties and protections for all its citizens, regardless of race or national origin. Civil rights for the twenty-first century must be prominent on America's moral radar screen, a crucial element of a new dialogue of engagement.

What happened in the 1990s in California with Proposition 187, which cut benefits for immigrants, and Proposition 209, which banned affirmative action, is a sad commentary on civil rights. With backing from the Republican right led by the governor at the time Pete Wilson and black conservatives such as Ward Connerly, Proposition 209 passed, and today it remains a sore thumb in the struggle for fairness and justice. In passing Proposition 209, misinformed voters cut off access to public-sector education, employment, and contracting to those who had been historically denied such opportunities—minorities and women. The 9th Circuit Court of Appeal upheld the constitutionality of Proposition 209 in August 1997, and the U.S. Supreme Court declined to hear the case subsequently that year. Three years later, the Supreme Court of the State of California further affirmed the constitutionality of Proposition 209 in a case involving the City of San Jose and Hi-Voltage Wire Works.

What happened in Florida in the 2000 presidential elections, in which many voters of African American descent were denied their rights to participate in the electoral process, is a national scandal. The Supreme Court of Florida, recognizing the sanctity of the fundamental right to vote, sided with the disenfranchised citizens of the state. Following a protracted legal battle between the Democratic candidate Vice President Al Gore, and the Republican candidate Texas Governor George W. Bush, the nation's Supreme Court overturned the decision of the Florida Court in a 5-4 vote ruling. December 2000 will go down in history for the fact that the conservative majority in the Rehnquist court chose a wrong path. It may not have mattered who won the election, so long as all the votes that were cast for that election were counted. No one knows the motivations for the decision of the conservative majority in the nation's highest court, but history may well judge them harshly for fueling the charge that when it comes to matters concerning the rights of the nation's black community, the courts have often been timid.

I agree with my good friend Omar Pela that "if there is a single Republican in this country who feigns indignation at the realization that blacks and immigrant groups vote overwhelmingly for Democrats, they know this constituency group little, and themselves even less."[59] Why should Republicans be surprised, Pela asks, at the voting patterns of these groups after Propositions 187 and 209? Why should anyone be surprised with black voting patterns when the only ones who came to their defense in the 2000 elections were those who called for their votes to count? In state after state, there have been systematic efforts to roll back the gains of the past. And the civil rights community has watched and walked as if there is no sense of urgency. Without dogged pressure and consistent public agitation on the part of black America, Hispanic America, Asian America, Native America, and other minority communities, as well as the civil rights community, there can be few or no gains for civil rights.

Perhaps, black America should be at the forefront of the struggle, but they cannot go it alone any longer. The Civil Rights doorway must expand to include other groups. Given its compelling history, black America offers the moral underpinnings of the struggles for civil rights. In the annals of American history, no single ethnic or racial group has endured the kind of human indignities suffered by American blacks—from the experience of slavery to slavery's enduring legacies. Despite the exploitation and the indignities, black America has learned forgiveness, and has left positive footprints on the watery sands of the American experience—in education, entertainment, sports, science, and technology. And black Americans have served gallantly in America's wars, including the war to defeat totalitarianism in Europe.

One must not overlook either the enslavement of the indigenous people by the Spanish or the continuing of nearly non-human status for Native American Indians and Latinos in the early days of the Southwest, not to mention the Chinese laborers, and other imported "workers" in our history.

At the end of the twentieth century, news accounts carried cover stories of adventures in science, of Einstein, and others, of remarkable technological breakthroughs and feats, all in celebration of humankind's achievements and rendezvous with destiny during that century. For black America, however, the story of humankind is not about the adventures in education, entertainment, sports, science, and technology. It is not about the rise and defeat of totalitarianism in Europe. These are important occurrences, but for black America, the fight for freedom and access represents, undeniably, the most meaningful struggle of the twentieth century, and indeed of its nearly four hundred years of servitude in America.

There is a long list of freedom fighters and leaders for civil rights— Marcus Garvey, Frederick Douglass, Sojourner Truth, W. E. B. Du Bois, Malcom X, and countless others, past and present, but I know of no single individual who provided a more significant national voice and moral fiber to the freedom struggles in America than Dr. Martin Luther King, Jr. He stands tall among the pre-eminent drivers of change in the struggle for human dignity.

King's Message

The substance of King's message was simple: "We must meet the forces of hate with the power of love; we must meet physical force with soul force. Our aim must never be to defeat or humiliate the white man, but to win his friendship and understanding.[60]" King came to national and international prominence at one of the most difficult times in America's history—an America that treated African Americans as second-class citizens. There were countless legal, psychological, and structural impediments in the educational, social, and economic arena. The young King immediately became the drum major for hope in an environment of hopelessness.

Somewhere in Montgomery, Alabama in 1955, a black woman, a seamstress by the name of Rosa Parks, had decided to ignore one of those psychological and structural impediments. She had become tired of the constant assault on her dignity and humanity. And so on that fateful day she refused to give up her seat on a segregated bus to a white passenger. The existing law required her to do so, and when she refused to comply, she was arrested. It was an unjust law. An unjust law "gives the segregator a false sense of superiority and the segregated a false sense of inferiority," King wrote in his now famous "Letter from Birmingham Jail,"[61] addressed to eight of his fellow clergy—Bishop C. C. J. Carpenter, Bishop Joseph Durick, Bishop Paul Hardin, Bishop Holan Harmon, Rabbi Hilton Grafman, the Reverend George Murray, the Reverend Edward Ramage, and the Reverend Earl Stallings. He continued,

> You express a great deal of anxiety over our willingness to break laws. This is certainly a legitimate concern. Since we so diligently urge people to obey the Supreme Court's decision of 1954 outlawing segregation in public schools, at first glance it may seem rather paradoxical for us consciously to break laws. One may ask: How can you advocate breaking some laws and obeying others? The answer lies in the fact that there are two types of laws: just and unjust. I would be the brat to advocate obeying just laws. One has not only a legal, but a moral responsibility to obey just laws. Conversely, one has a moral responsibility to disobey unjust laws.

King went further in his letter to provide several examples of just or unjust laws. For instance, "An unjust law is a code that a numerical or power majority group compels a minority group to obey but does not make binding on itself. This is difference made legal. By the same token, a just law is a code that a majority compels a minority to follow and that it is willing to follow itself. This is sameness made legal," he noted.

Desegregation Hurt Black America

There is an on-going undercurrent of debate in black America today regarding King's message of desegregation and its impact on black America's economic and social life. Some have made the case that desegregation hurt black affirmation. Had black America focused on political freedom and access to economic resources, rather than on racial desegregation or integration, black economic and social life, the argument goes, would have been much better. Indeed, there is no question that most black economic progress emerged during the days of segregation. All of the historically black colleges, for example, which served black America well, emerged in the days of segregation. Today, several of these institutions are struggling to survive.

In fact, since desegregation, there have emerged very few major black institutions of significance, in particular in media and entertainment. The desegregation efforts may have worked well in some areas, but in many others, such as in the educational system, it shifted needed dollars away from black schools to white schools. There is something wrong with the belief that one's reference point for excellence revolves around participation at the table of integration. Nothing can be further from the truth. Perhaps, in pursuing freedom and access, Martin Luther King, Jr. went too far in choosing racial desegregation rather than black affirmation and economic empowerment.

But placed in his historical context, King was a visionary and tactician. As a visionary, he saw that there was a ceiling on how far blacks could excel in the U. S. Thus, he believed that freedom and access through integration was the only way, at least at that moment, to remove that ceiling. Integration would help demystify white America's perceptions about black inferiority. Among blacks, there was no doubt that they could excel. The doubts about black excellence were not internal, but external—in the minds of white America. The more that white America would learn of black America through integration, the more that white America would respect black America. This appeared to be King's reasoning for integration. Everything else would then follow. It was akin to Kwame Nkrumah's message from Ghana to African liberation fighters in the 1960s: seek first the political kingdom, and economic independence would follow thereafter.

There are significant areas of national life in which the efforts to integrate provided equal access to African Americans, such as the Rosa Parks incident. King had traveled to Montgomery, Alabama, where he held discussions with like-minded leaders in the city. These discussions led to the formation of the Montgomery Improvement Association (MIA), with King as its president. On December 5, 1955, upon becoming the MIA's president, King applied the non-violence principles in the famous Montgomery bus boycott that economically paralyzed the city. As a tactician, King believed that civil disobedience grounded on a strong moral foundation would not be the only approach. Legal pressure deriving from constitutional authority would also be used.

On February 21, 1956, lawyers for the MIA filed a suit in U. S. District Court asking that Montgomery's segregation laws be declared unconstitutional. Less than four months later (June 4), the Court ruled in the MIA's favor. But the battle was not over as the case was appealed to the U. S. Supreme Court. On November 13, 1956, the Supreme Court, the highest court in the land, affirmed the decision of the lower court, and declared that Alabama's segregation laws were unconstitutional. For the first time in the history of Alabama, public buses were desegregated, and African Americans could sit anywhere on the bus like every other bus passenger. It was a major victory for human dignity, and it was a victory that marked the beginning of the modern civil rights movement. King had championed it (with support from both whites and blacks), and he was only twenty-five years old when he began to lead the movement.

From then on, King led campaign after campaign in the streets of America to end racial segregation and to secure dignity for African Americans. And he did so, successfully, with a simple philosophy—change through nonviolence, a philosophy he had learned from Mahatma Ghandi of India, whose message of passive resistance changed the face of India during the dark days of colonialism.

Clearly, television lent reach to King's voice. For the first time, Americans of all shades witnessed the ugly events from their living rooms as they unfolded on television. King became the conscience of the nation as men and women of goodwill, black and white, joined in the crusade for which he was named Time's 1964 Man of the Year. Then, on December 10, 1964, he traveled to Oslo, Norway to receive the Nobel Prize for Peace, the youngest-ever recipient of such prize at the time. He was only thirty-five years old. King also spoke with eloquence on matters of national and international significance such as the Vietnam War, although his criticism of America's role there did not receive blessings at the highest levels of the American political and intelligence establishment.

While King's work was centered in the U. S., his influence and impact were global. He unmasked the evil of racism, taught us about the power of forgiveness, and demonstrated that the content of one's character, not necessarily one's race, should matter in our national ethic. "There is some good in the worst of us and some evil in the best of us. When we discover this, we are less prone to hate our enemies," he wrote in his book, Strength to Love.[62] What is the message of today's civil rights movement and what is their approach? It is not quite clear.

An Uncertain Agenda

The trouble with the struggle for civil rights in America since King's death can be viewed from three perspectives. First, there is the absence of a clear national agenda for both political and economic progress for black America. Second, there is the absence of a clear mechanism or approach for pursuing both the political and economic goals. Third, there is no serious discussion regarding how best to gain and sustain the interest of a new generation of black youth born after the struggles of the 1960s who appear to have no understanding of the sacrifice that got them where they are today. Inherent in this perspective is the growing but more troubling perception among black youth that the civil rights agenda may be a relic of the past.

After all, how does one explain the seemingly national acquiescence by black civil rights leaders nationally to unjust laws which have had a devastating impact on young people—laws or policies such as the ones that promote racial profiling in law enforcement practices, for example, the Rockefeller drug laws in New York and California's "three-strikes" law, which are creating a permanent underclass of young black men.

The Rockefeller drug laws were enacted in 1973 when Nelson Rockefeller was governor of New York. The laws require harsh prison terms for the possession or sale of relatively small amounts of drugs. The harshest provision of the laws mandates a judge to impose a prison term of no less than fifteen years to life for any person convicted of selling two ounces or possessing four ounces of a narcotic substance, regardless of the circumstances of the offense or the individual's character or background. Many people have called for the repeal of the laws because it targets mostly minorities.

We have allowed the emergence of a prison-industrial complex, spending billions of dollars for the purposes of incarcerating young offenders. In the past twenty years, New York State has opened thirty-eight prisons, (at the rate of nearly two prisons per year) all in rural, mainly white areas, all represented by Republican state senators. From 1988–98, the state spending on its prison system increased by $761 million, while spending on the State and City Universities of New York decreased by approximately $615 million.[63]

In a period of ten years alone, California, which has the third largest penal system in the world, spent over $10 billion on building fifteen new prisons. Between 1984–94, the state hired 26,000 new employees to guard 112,000 new prisoners, at the same time as it was cutting 8,000 jobs from state colleges and universities. Today, the number of black men in the state's prison system (roughly 42,000) surpasses the number of black men in college by a ratio of four to one![64] The state's "three-strikes" law, formally known as Proposition 184, which doubles sentences for second offenders and decrees twenty-five years to life for three-time offenders, is expected to worsen an already crowded prison population and places additional pressures on the state's already limited resources. Governor Gray Davis in his 2003 budget proposed a new state prison at San Quentin that will cost taxpayers millions of dollars. In December 2006, his successor Governor Arnold Schwarzenegger proposed a prison overhaul that would cost $10 billion dollars of state money.

The independent RAND Corporation has noted in a study that "higher education and other government services would have to fall by more than 40 percent over the next eight years"[65] to fully support the implementation of Proposition 184. RAND estimates suggest that by the end of 2002, the state government was spending more money to keep people in prison than putting people through college, a consequence of the three-strikes law. Yet the state marched forward with implementing the law.

The Cost of More Prisons

Correctional peace officers receive salaries starting at $3,050–$5,188 per month, depending on assigned duties, plus paid medical, dental, and vision benefits, paid vacation, sick leave, retirement contributions, and they may be eligible for education and fitness incentives. Without promotion, these positions top out at a range of $6,144–$7,772 based upon increments of 5 percent increases each six months while in training and annually thereafter.

The results are an annual salary range of \$36,600–\$93,264 plus benefits for a high-school education plus six months of community-college-level academy training.[66] Beginning officers have been known to earn twice their annual salary in overtime payments annually. By comparison, in California public universities, tenure-track, new-hire assistant professors with Ph.D. degrees start at about \$48,000, depending on location and field, and top out at about \$90,000 plus paid medical, dental, and vision benefits, sick leave, and retirement contributions before promotion.[67]

It may be said that the California Correctional Peace Officers Association, the prison guard union, is the single most affluent and influential lobbying organization in California, more influential than the university professors or the clergy of the state.

Who Suffers under these Laws?

African Americans have suffered most under the laws, many arrested for infractions involving the sale of marijuana, a drug common in the black community. There is a less harsh disposition in the law for possession of cocaine and methamphetamines, drugs that are common among white users. Data released in 2004 by the Justice Policy Institute show that African-Americans, who make up 10 percent of California's population, accounted for nearly 45 percent of the three-strikes cases in the state, thirteen times the rate for white offenders.[68] Because of this apalling law, a permanent underclass of young black men is emerging—in Oakland, Los Angeles, and elsewhere. They are more likely to end up in prison than to go to college. We are creating a Frankenstein monster for which citizens ultimately will pay a price.

The Average Daily Prison Population, calendar year 2006, of the California Department of Corrections and Rehabilitation (CCDR), reports that the quarterly average for October through December reached 172,925 adults.[69] Reporting by ethnicity shows Hispanic 38 percent, black 29 percent, white 27 percent, other 6 percent.[70] Because in the U. S. Census, Hispanics may be of varying racial identification, including white, black, other, and two or more races, it is difficult to make a direct comparison with CCDR adult population figures, but the U. S. Census estimates the 2006 California population by race and ethnicity as Hispanic or Latino 35.9 percent, black or African American 6.2 percent, white 59.8 percent, Asian 12 percent, American Indian and Alaska Native (AI/AN) 0.7 percent, Native Hawaiian or Pacific Islander (NH/PI) 0.4 percent, other race 17.3 percent, two or more races 3.3 percent.[71] This information is summarized in figure 1.

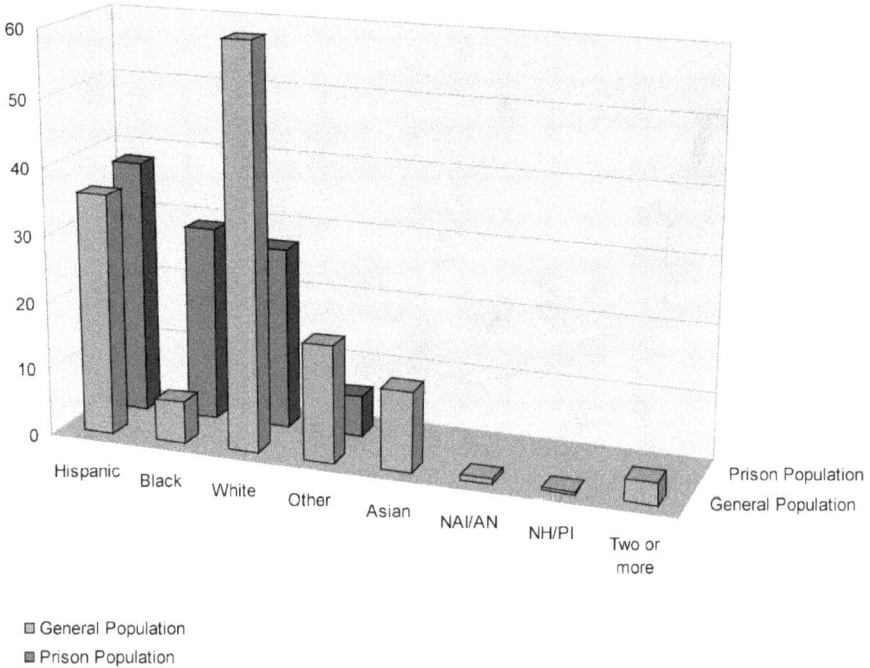

Figure 1: Adult California prison population compared to total population–2006[72]

The Division of Juvenile Justice reports 2,509 juveniles in custody and 3,072 on parole. Reporting by ethnicity shows Hispanic 51 percent, African American 31 percent, white 13 percent, Asian 2 percent, Filipino 1 percent, Native American 1 percent, Pacific Islander 1 percent, and other 1%.[73] Kids Data reports for 2005 California's juvenile population distribution was Hispanic/Latino 47.7 percent, African American/black 7.2 percent, Caucasian/white 31.4 percent, Asian 9.4 percent, Native American 0.8 percent, Pacific Islander 0.4 percent, multiracial 3.4 percent.[74] These data are summarized in figure 2.

To believe that the expansion of the prison-industrial complex is our only way to address misbehavior not only is a serious failure of our criminal justice policy, but is also an indictment of the economic and social policies that produced, in part, the dislocations that give birth to the criminal behavior in the first place. Democrats and Republicans, conservatives, moderates, liberals, and independents must take responsibility for this breakdown.

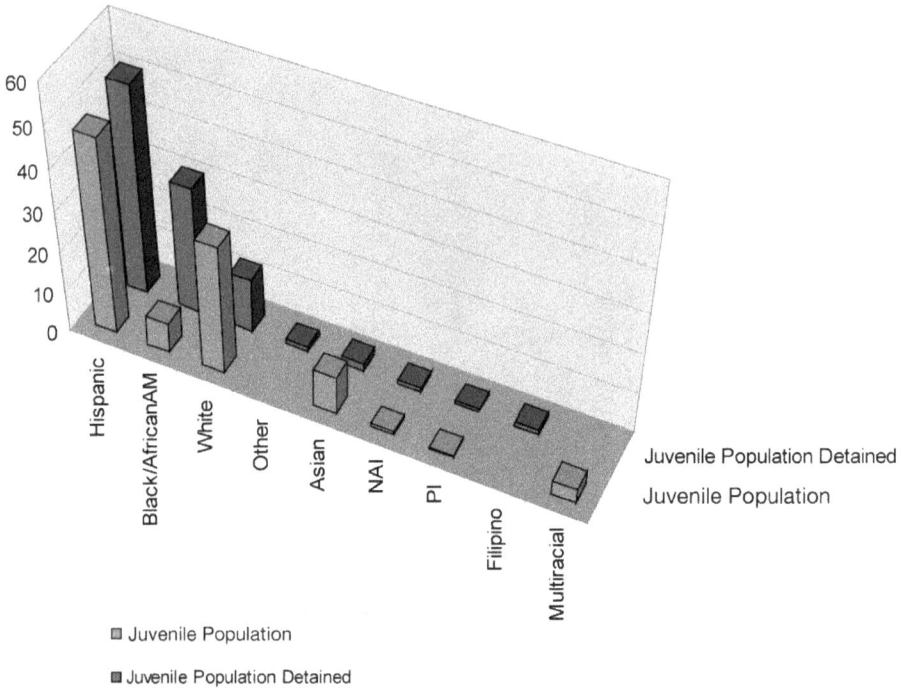

Figure 2: Juvenile California prison population compared to total California children population

The Failure of Social Welfare

The Rockefeller drug laws, the three-strikes law, and other similar laws or policies merit resistance. Randall Robinson of TransAfrica demonstrated strength and courage in the 1990s when he went on a hunger strike to protest the Clinton administration's refusal to deal with human rights abuses by the military junta in Haiti, and he succeeded in causing the administration to change course.

Yet the politics of inaction, coupled with an uncertain agenda on the part of civil rights leaders, on matters of great significance in the domestic civil rights arena in the U. S. remains baffling. The inaction is exacerbated by a national audience of American people who have refused to recognize the ultimate dangers posed by such laws as New York's Rockefeller drug laws or California's three-strikes laws.

The impact of these laws is felt mostly in minority communities, where the economic and social dislocations are quite high. Juvenile justice literature indicates that poverty and high rates of unemployment in inner cities are correlated to arrest, intake, adjudication, and disposition with differential outcomes leading to confinement for those with lower socioeconomic status. While there are differences in patterns of offence across racial groups, the literature also provides clear indications of race differentials in justice processing, patterns of policing, and racial bias in the juvenile justice system. We remain slaves to the "nimby" phenomenon: if the problem is not in my backyard (nimby), it does not matter. We remain silent in the face of a ticking time-bomb of rage in young blacks—daily victims of a society that has marked them out as criminals because of the color of their skin. An uncertain agenda and an uncertain approach certainly consign, in the minds of these young people, the civil rights project to the scrapbook of history.

We remain silent also at the disproportionate numbers of minority children in America's foster care system and the juvenile justice set-up. While African American children, for example, constitute only 17 percent of the nation's young citizens, 42 percent of all children in the nation's foster care system are African American. In the big inner cities such as Chicago, San Francisco, New York, and San Diego, "the foster care population is almost exclusively Black, with a smaller percentage of Latino children, and a tiny fraction of white children."[75] As Dorothy Roberts of Northwestern University Law School writes, black children are separated from their parents with relative ease and are the most likely of any group to be disrupted by child protection authorities. Punishment, rather than rehabilitation, as in the case of fourteen-year old Lionel Tate, who was sentenced to life without the possibility of parole for killing six-year-old Tiffany Eunick, has become the theme song of our approach to addressing juvenile misbehavior. When this situation explodes, what happened in Los Angeles after the Rodney King incident will seem like child's play. Increasingly, it appears in California and many other places that the system is not about "justice" but rather control and punishment.

Today's civil rights organizations and leaders, while numerous, have failed to grasp the enormity of the continuing challenges to the gains of the modern civil rights movement, including the challenges posed by the explosion of the prison-industrial complex. They must accept some blame for their inaction and the uncertain agenda. Toni Humber of California State Polytechnic University, Pomona has argued that historically, those black men and women who have spoken out have been hanged, castrated, exiled, discredited, imprisoned, executed, or assassinated.[76] The atmosphere of fear that has engulfed the civil rights community, she argues, may account for the uncertain agenda and today's politics of inaction or the politics of caution.

Whether the present state of inaction or caution is a consequence of fear or of a changing political landscape, today's civil rights leaders remain unsure of what the civil rights agenda of the twenty-first century ought to be and of the direction and the methods for pursuing the agenda. King's simple message was freedom and access, and the methods were legal battles in the halls of justice and street protests grounded on the gospel of nonviolence. He was unshakable and fearless in his devotion to justice, enormously committed to racial desegregation, and convinced that civil disobedience coupled with a well-designed legal strategy was the paramount approach. Where is the agenda and where is the approach of today's civil rights community on questions of civil rights and economic justice?

7

THE BLACK PROBLEM

The nonethnic consumer is more attractive. Clients should be steered toward radio stations with broader-based audiences. Advertisers want prospects, not suspects.

Excerpts from a training memo to advertising staff

I want to say this about my state [Mississippi]. When Strom Thurmond ran for president, we voted for him. We're proud of it. And if the rest of the country had followed our lead, we wouldn't have had all these problems over all these years, either.

Senator Trent Lott

We must clean our house. There are too many today, white and black, on the left and right, on the street corners and the radio waves, who seek to sow division for their own purposes. To them I say: No more. We must be one … We dare not tolerate the existence of two Americas.

President Bill Clinton

My nation's journey toward justice has not been easy and it is not over. The racial bigotry fed by slavery did not end with slavery or with segregation, and many of the issues that still trouble America have roots in the bitter experience of other times.

President George W. Bush

The Black Problem

Something strange happened a while ago that reaffirmed my conviction that America has a black problem. It was the famous December 16, 2002 interview of Senator Trent Lott by Ed Gordon on Black Entertainment Television (BET). Earlier that month, at a Capitol Hill celebration to mark the 100th birthday of retiring Senator Strom Thurmond, Lott had commented as follows:

"I want to say this about my state: When Strom Thurmond ran for president, we voted for him. We're proud of it. And if the rest of the country had followed our lead, we wouldn't have had all these problems over all these years, either."[77] It was a statement most people perceived as laced with racist connotations, given Senator Thurmond's history as an arch segregationist. The uproar that followed the remarks forced Lott to go on national television, including the Black media, to apologize, and to completely reverse his long-standing opposition to one of the most divisive issues in American society today—affirmative action.

I watched the BET interview with astonishment. Lott's reversal was a near-death conversion presented in an hour of tribulation in a manner that was inconsistent with the man's traditional position on an issue he and many in his party describe (albeit wrongly) as racial quotas. In this interview, Senator Lott also told Ed Gordon that he would vote today in support of a national holiday honoring the legacy of Dr. Martin Luther King, Jr., America's most celebrated civil rights messenger. In 1983 the man from Mississippi had voted against the King holiday because, as he said, he did not understand the significance of King in the nation's life. I watched in disbelief, not that one cannot have a Paul-on-the-road-to-Damascus change of heart concerning a people persecuted, but because the senior senator's remarks (as most people, including honest Republicans, admitted) defied years of recorded behaviors opposed to the civil rights agenda.

Months after that momentous interview, I sat in my university's ballroom to listen to Ed Gordon as he recounted his feelings to a packed audience of students, faculty, staff, and community members. Speaking at events marking the beginning of Black History Month at our campus, the veteran anchorman wondered what else the famed senator could support in the effort to maintain his grip on power. Perhaps, he queried, with no disrespect intended, a national holiday for the fallen African American rap star Tupac Shakur? I will return to Lott later in this chapter.

Lott's remarks at retiring Senator Thurmond's birthday celebration were not a blatant act of cross-burning to intimidate and demonstrate hate. What was different this time was that the subtle racist attitudes embedded in his message did not go unnoticed. If America is to move beyond race, it must confront the continuing subtle racist attitudes against its minority black population. These subtle racist attitudes—still prevalent in various arenas of public and social life—I call the black problem. In the history of the U. S., different categories of persons have been a problem of some sort in America's march toward a more perfect union: Native American Indians, Irish, Germans, Italians, Jews, Japanese. Early-arriving immigrants resented later-arriving immigrants and worked hard to make life difficult for them, ironically in a nation created and continually redefined primarily by voluntary immigration. But the resentment against these groups by no means matches the resentment against American blacks, in particular black males. This resentment sadly continues till this day even with every law imaginable on the books.

The black problem is particularly unique and complex because it reveals an unspoken irritant: a general perception that black people are a thorn in the flesh of every racial group in America. Each racial group sees them as troublemakers, aggressive, hostile, loud-mouthed, violent, and poor. Each racial group sees them as inferior, ignorant, and lazy. Each racial group sees them as arrogant. Each racial group's portrait of criminal behavior is always painted in black. And each racial group perceives American blacks as using the notion of victim-hood to constantly seek handouts from the government rather than work as hard as other groups. If there is one area of near unanimity among all racial groups in America, it lies regrettably in the black problem—the common resentment of the black person. Yet everything we know from the history of our country tells us that we cannot build a new vision of America unless we commit our nation and ourselves to removing the lingering relics of this racial nightmare. But first we must be candid with ourselves and acknowledge the existence and persistence of this problem. Second, we must identify the nature of this problem, including some specific arenas of our national life where the problem remains. Third, we must identify some strategies for dealing with the challenges posed by the black problem.

There is no doubt that the common resentment of black people is historical and enduring. Our nation's history is littered with pages of anti-black feeling, negative perceptions, and stereotypes since 1619 when twenty blacks were brought to Jamestown as the first set of slaves to arrive North America. An excellent examination of attitudes toward American blacks from the sixteenth century through the early years of the founding of the republic can be found in Winthrop Jordan's classic work White over Black.[78] From the period when abolitionists (most of them white) were active in the struggle to end slavery, to the period of the Civil War between the North and the South when Abraham Lincoln led the nation in the battle which resulted in the end of slavery, until this day, the common resentment remains a staple in America's racial tête-à-tête.

Looking back at the nation's long and troubled racial history, it is impossible to find one black person who has not been exposed to the widespread antipathy against African Americans: Frederick Douglass, Booker T. Washington, W. E. B. Du Bois, Malcolm X, John Lewis, Barbara Jordan, Jesse Jackson, Thurgood Marshall, Colin Powell, Bill Cosby, Oprah Winfrey, Clarence Thomas, Maya Angelou, Condoleeza Rice, Toni Morrison, Johnnie Cochran, Cornell West, and so on. America's workplaces, schools, and malls, banks, car dealerships, and shoe stores, among others, offer platforms for those determined to unleash the new resentment regardless of laws in the books that bar such conduct. We have made progress in removing from the books some of the pernicious legal barriers to building a genuine American community, but we have not coupled it with a national will and the leadership to educate and to change the minds and attitudes of our citizenry. More than three hundred and eighty-five years after the first blacks set foot in Jamestown, the black problem remains in the American psyche and landscape, manifested now in different, more subtle, but troubling forms that call into question America's commitment to a more perfect union.

The New Resentment

In the summer of 1994, I was stopped by a police officer while taking a walk around my new neighborhood in Sacramento, California's capital. The officer, who had trailed me in his car for about five minutes, finally stopped and inquired from me if I lived around the block. I responded in the affirmative, and wanted to know why he asked. He said he simply wanted to know. I paused for a moment, and continued my walk, at which point he drove off. I was unsure how to interpret that interaction.

One cannot begin to imagine the countless numbers of black people—influential or ordinary—who are pulled over by law enforcement personnel for flimsy reasons, in what many have called "driving while black." The late

Johnnie Cochran told of a similar experience with police in a BET profile on him a few years ago. Cornel West recalled a similar experience with police when he was stopped a few years ago on charges of trafficking cocaine while driving from New York to teach at Williams College. "When I told the police officer I was a professor of religion, he replied 'Yeh, and I'm the Flying Nun. Let's go, nigger!'" [79] The charges turned out to be concocted. Black parents tell their teenage children to stop, to pull over and to completely raise their hands in full view, if and when they are asked to do so by law enforcement. This way, they can stay alive. This type of experience remains common among blacks in most cities across America in their encounters with law enforcement. Too many black youths have fallen victim to the raw use of power by irresponsible police officers. And too many irresponsible police officers have gotten away with these behaviors. The thinking today in the black community and among black parents in particular is simple: if an all-white jury in California's Simi Valley could set free the Los Angeles police officers captured on video as they brutally assaulted Rodney King, then no black person is immune from police brutality. Certainly, there are many police officers I know who are doing a fine job to protect life and property, but they have a responsibility to help sift from their midst those officers who cast a blight on police work.

Not long ago, Bernadette Park, professor of psychology at the University of Boulder, in Colorado, conducted a study of subtle forms of the new resentment or racism in law enforcement, and found, worryingly, that "the threshold to decide to shoot is set lower for African Americans than for whites."[80] In a video-game study designed to show whether there is a differential association of violence with blacks or with whites, Park instructed subjects to shoot only when human targets in the game were armed. The results of the study showed that police officers made more errors when confronted with images of black men carrying objects like cell phones or cameras than when faced with similarly unarmed white men. In one study in which participants were primarily white, the subjects were also quicker to fire on black men with guns than on white men with guns. In the past thirty years, we have seen countless studies in which black men were more likely to be perceived as violent than whites, even when the actions being performed were the same.

A study conducted by researchers at the University of Chicago Graduate School of Business and the Massachusetts Institute of Technology provide a frightening new picture of subtle forms of resentment against blacks in corporate America. The study,[81] conducted over a one-year period, found African Americans with ethnic-sounding names were more likely to be the first casualties in the application screening processes, and were therefore denied employment opportunities. Researchers sent a random selection of 5,000 qualified resumes to 1,300 openings for sales, clerical, and management jobs advertised in both the Boston Globe and the Chicago Tribune. One set of resumes was given names common among African Americans such as

Tamika, Ebony, Aisha, Kareem, Tyrone, and Rasheed, and the other set of resumes was given names common to whites such as Neil, Brett, Emily, and Anne. All of the names were gleaned from birth certificates. The result of the study indicated that applicants with white-sounding names were 50 percent more likely to be invited for job interviews. The most disturbing result of the study is that "even though all the resumes were qualified, one of each set, African-American and White, was slightly stronger than the others in the same racial group. But even then the stronger African-American-named applicant was less likely to be interviewed than the stronger White-named applicant."[82]

In 1998, Clifton Castell published a striking study of the new resentment in America's integrated classrooms, and concluded that African American students continue to be treated less favorably by teachers.[83] Research variables examined by Castell included amount of praise given for both correct and incorrect answers, hints provided to assist in answers, rephrasing of questions, and calling on students by name. Male Caucasian students, he found, received the highest levels of positive teacher contact, while African American males received the least favorable treatment from their teachers. Castell's work provides further support for decades of research since the1970s on the interface between student-teacher interactions and race in the classroom—research concluding that black students receive less attention, less praise, and are ignored and reprimanded more than their white counterparts. In explaining these variations, Castell notes that approximately 90 percent of teachers in integrated schools are Caucasian and female. Most of these teachers are from suburban communities, with little contact or experience with African American students or their backgrounds. Consequently, they tend to have low expectations for and tolerance of African American students, especially black males. The low expectations are informed by perceptual images engraved in the minds of the teachers since childhood. Perhaps, lacking exposure to the benefits of diversity, these teachers wreak psychological havoc on a generation of young black males, havoc that is injurious to their development orientation and their educational career, as well as their life choices.

Compounding the racial challenge in the classroom is the teachers' poor knowledge of African American cultural patterns and the communication styles that most African American students bring to the classrooms. Not understanding the culture and communication styles, teachers make faulty attributions and assessments that, over time, become injurious to the students' capacity to learn. The focus on understanding cultural patterns and communication styles is crucial to managing an integrated or multicultural classroom, and has been a central theme of the dialogue and workshops I have had with thousands of teachers on this subject in the past decade. Certainly teacher bias (whether conscious or unconscious) can impact students' self-esteem, motivation, and academic performance. The damage and loss to our society cannot be quantified. We end up producing half-baked citizens at the expense of our economy and way of life, setting them up for failure. We must treat all of our students as America's students, not as black students or white students, not as Asian students or Latino students, not as Native Americans or Pacific Islanders. But we must understand the cultural patterns and communication styles that they bring to the classroom, so that we can motivate them more effectively and teach them more efficiently. That is the challenge of today's knowledge economy.

I am reminded of the experience of my niece and her female friends in Washington, D. C. Whenever they went into a nearby local Chinese restaurant in the northwest section of the city, the owners would recoil in fear as if the young black women, all college students, had come to rob them. Whenever she walked into an elevator with her friends for a ride to the next floor, some white female patrons would stand in the corner, almost in visible fear, as they clutched their wallets tightly. Several years ago at my previous university, one Jewish student confided in tears that she always cringed, even on campus, whenever she saw herself in close proximity to blacks. The university environment, she shared with me, was her first serious experience with intercultural encounters. She had lived in a small community and went to schools that had few minorities. None was African-American. And she had not been exposed to their history, beyond what she saw on television. She had grown up to fear them.

Too many of our students have the same experience. The fault, however, is not in the students. In the new America that I speak of, the task of educators and teachers is to comprehensively prepare students for life and competent communication in an increasingly multicultural society. Students must now work not only with those who look exactly like them, but also with those who are different in many ways. We must inoculate our students against irrational fears and ethnocentric tendencies. That is our task as educators in a globalizing workplace.

New Resentment in Society

In 1991 Diane Sawyer of ABC presented a compelling portrait of the new resentment against blacks in numerous instances of business and social life in America. Using the beautiful city of St. Louis, Missouri as a test case, Sawyer sent two men, one black and one white, with similar backgrounds, to assess how much difference the color of one's skin still made in everyday life in America. From the search for housing, to purchasing a new car, buying shoes at the mall, looking for employment, to something as minor as getting a taxi cab for a ride home, both men received significantly disparate treatment. The black gentleman, in every instance, experienced discrimination. Emotionally drained from the experience, he remarked, "I cannot take off my black skin. I am going to remain black for the rest of my life."[84] Yet skin color remains an important consideration for employment, housing, and loan approval. Black Americans, notes Sawyer in the documentary, spend over $150 million more annually in interests on car loans than white Americans, because lenders do not see them as "sophisticated" customers.[85] Sawyer's video True Colors, which I have used frequently to engage my students in conversations about racial attitudes, is an excellent tool for demonstrating to those who may continue to be in denial about the nature and dynamic of the new resentment. In other words, those doubting or looking to see the subtleties or the form and shape of the new resentment will be well advised to look at this video. In practically every aspect of public and social life in America, we find increasing levels of the new forms of resentment. Many perceptions of it are supported by research. Several perceptions go unnoticed: in the placement of radio and television advertising, in the healthcare system, in mortgage lending. The list goes on.

A major study conducted in 1999 by the Federal Communications Commission (FCC) of 3,745 radio stations,[86] the first government study on discrimination in radio advertising, showed that stations aimed primarily at black and Hispanic audiences receive significantly less advertising revenue per listener than their white counterparts. While demographics and ratings affect advertising, the study found that minority-owned radio stations were made to offer deeper discounts in exchange for ads than their mainstream counterparts.

Not long ago, the Institute of Medicine (IOM) released the results of a ten-year study[87] commissioned by Congress to assess racial and ethnic differences in health care. The results showed glaring heath-care disparities between minorities and whites caused by bias, stereotyping, and discrimination at the individual, institutional, and health-care system levels. While citing poverty, inadequate education, lack of health insurance, inferior living conditions, and lack of access to quality health care as additional causes of the disparities, IOM found that minority groups, in particular African Americans, were less likely than white Americans to receive even routine medical procedures in such areas as coronary artery bypass surgery and kidney dialysis.

In 1989, the Atlanta Journal Constitution published a Pulitzer-Prize winning series entitled "The Color of Money," highlighting serious evidence of discrimination in mortgage lending by the Atlanta-based Decatur Federal Savings & Loan.[88] The series resulted in a case against the company by the U. S. Justice Department. In fact, because of discrepancies in lending practices from depository and nondepository institutions, Congress enacted a variety of laws beginning in the 1960s that makes it illegal for lenders to discriminate against historically disadvantaged groups such as women and minorities. The Fair Housing Act of 1968, the Equal Credit Opportunity Act of 1974, the Home Mortgage Disclosure Act of 1975 and the1989 revisions, as well as the Community Reinvestment Act of 1977, have all been designed to prevent discrimination in lending practices. Nearly four decades since the passing of the Fair Housing Act, we continue to find evidence of discriminatory lending practices by lending institutions against minorities, especially African Americans. Disparate treatment has been found in three specific areas: differences in loan denial rates, differences in loan default rates, and geographic redlining, i.e., factoring the racial composition of the neighborhood.[89]

One would think that nearly twenty years after the Atlanta Journal Constitution publication the situation would be different. That is not the case. Indeed, a recent study found that minority homeowners, regardless of their income, were more likely than whites to get high-interest loans when they refinanced their mortgages. Data collected from more than 7,800 financial institutions in the U. S. show that African Americans in Washington, D. C. alone accounted for 40.48 percent of sub-prime loans in the district in 2007, "compared with 26.39 percent of all refinance loans made to Latino homeowners, and just 9.34 percent made to white homeowners."[90] In addition, a recent study by two Oregon State University faculty Jonathan Kaplan and Andrew Valls found that "a large fraction of the black/white 'wealth gap' is related to the very different home ownership rates of white and black Americans, and the differences in the value of homes owned by black and white Americans," a "situation created by government programs that deliberately made it much more difficult for black Americans to acquire homes at the same time they made it much easier for white Americans to acquire homes."[91] Furthermore, Kaplan and Valls found that blacks "were almost completely excluded from benefiting from these loans because the FHA assigned 'risk'. Ratings to neighborhoods, based on various demographic factors, especially race. Mixed and predominantly black neighborhoods were rated as 'riskier' and were generally not eligible for FHA loans."[92] There have been some discussions about risk factors and profit motives as shaping lending habits, but the laws are equally clear in insisting that lenders not use stereotypes or negative statistics about an applicant's group to assess the applicant's creditworthiness.

In the arena of child welfare, the story is the same. In her compelling examination of America's child welfare system, Dorothy Roberts of the Northwestern University Law School concludes that the very structure of child welfare is fundamentally flawed.[93] Instead of targeting the systemic reasons for family hardship to prevent child maltreatment, it lays the blame on individual parents' failings after a crisis has occurred. Instead of supporting families, it punishes them by taking children from their homes for placement in foster care. The result of this defective structure is that children of color, especially black children, are taken from their parents in disproportionate numbers. Disproportionality exists when there is a difference between the proportion of children of a particular racial or ethnic group in the child welfare system and the proportion of children in that particular racial or ethnic group in the general population.[94] While black children constitute only 17 percent of the nation's children, they make up 42 percent of children in foster care. Moreover, "most white children who enter the system are permitted to stay with their families, whereas most Black children are taken away from theirs. Foster care is the main 'service' that state agencies provide to Black children brought to their attention. Government authorities appear to believe that maltreatment of Black children results from pathologies intrinsic to their homes and that helping them requires dislocating them from their families."[95]

Most experts note that the current approach to child welfare, which consigns an alarming number of black children to state intervention and supervision, essentially weakens black family and community ties and reinforces racial inequality and the perception that the system is patently unfair. Many scholars now agree that the child welfare system focuses more on the removal of the child so as to punish the parent rather than working to preserve or reunify parent and child. Instead of seeking ways to assist the failing parent through recovery, the system ironically helps to destroy the family. Yet each player in the system strives to do good work and to be fair.

One is reminded of the child whose mother sent him to school with the admonition to be good and to do good always.[96] Each day, he went by a small river that cut across from his home. One day on his way home from school, he noticed what appeared to be a fish "drowning" in this river. Quickly, he tried to help and to save the fish from drowning. He managed and succeeded in grabbing the fish and setting it down on the ground to dry. Excited with his accomplishment, he rushed home to tell his mother. Shocked at what her son had done, both mother and child rushed back to the scene only to find the fish dead. If only the child knew the "culture" of the fish, he would have responded differently. Most social workers mean well and indeed strive to be fair. However, in their effort to save the child from harm, real or imagined, they offer intervention strategies that disregard the culture of the both parent and child, and ultimately inflict greater harm to the child's well-being.

I agree with Roberts that the child welfare system in the U. S. is designed and operated in a way that invites bias and unfair habits against minority families. For example, Roberts writes, "vague definitions of neglect, unbridled discretion, and lack of training [in cultural competencies] form a dangerous combination in the hands of caseworkers charged with deciding the fate of families. Child neglect is sometimes defined broadly as any parental failure that presents an imminent risk of serious harm."[97] The result is that across the country, black parents lose their children to the state, leading some scholars, including myself, to question what role race plays in this process, or is it that black families cannot rear children?

In a very interesting piece published in the American Journal of Orthopsychiatry, Ann Garland and her colleagues propose what they call the "visibility hypothesis" to further explain why there is a higher probability for children of color to be placed in foster care "when living in a geographic area where they are relatively less represented (i.e., less 'visible')."[98] Drawing from data from the child welfare system in California, Garland and her colleagues concluded that visibility increases the chances for minority contact and placement with the system for two reasons: first, child protective services agencies, given prevailing negative perceptions and attitudes about underrepresented groups, are more likely to investigate these groups, and second, these underrepresented groups generally do not have the support networks that could fend off any investigation from the child welfare system.

In the past ten years, I have worked with the child welfare system in California and some of its related entities to develop methods for integrating fairness and equity in the state's child welfare system. In the first major report presented to state's Stakeholders Summit in May 2002, in Anaheim, California, I noted on behalf of the Working Group on Fairness and Equity that

> The flawed and defective structure under which the (child welfare) system currently operates increases the potential for differential processing and raises profound questions as to the fairness of the system. At a minimum, the fact that caseworkers have considerable discretion in the determination of how and what types of charges to place against an alleged offender complicates the interpretation of the disparities in the system and presents wide-ranging implications for fairness. Are some families from particular backgrounds either committing more serious offenses with regard to child maltreatment, neglect and abuse, or are they being charged with more serious offenses regarding child maltreatment, neglect and abuse because of their backgrounds (culture, economic status, immigrant status, race, ethnicity, or sexual/affective orientation, etc)? In the former instance, we have what Lockhart et al. (1990) call "understandable disparity." In the second instance, we have discrimination—and a system that is patently lacking in fairness.[99]

Disparate treatment also extends to the judicial arena. Numerous surveys show that the country's most vocal minority holds a very poor impression of the nation's courts.[100] The sentiment in black America is that in cases of inter-racial crime involving a black defendant and a white plaintiff, the defendant will be treated more harshly than in a situation where the defendant is white. Similarly, the sentiment suggests that a white defendant will be treated less harshly than the black defendant in a crime where the victim is black.

Recent data on juvenile case processing across the country showed that a greater proportion of minorities, especially African Americans, received harsher disposition at each successive stage of the juvenile justice system from arrest, through intake, adjudication, and disposition. Even after controlling for such variables as seriousness of offense and history of crime, findings show clear indications of race differentials in justice processing. National research examined by my colleagues and me under a contract with the Sacramento Criminal Justice Cabinet points to the following:

- the largest overrepresentation is to be found at the arrest and disposition stages;

- among minorities, African American youths were more likely to be overrepresented at every stage: twice as likely to be sentenced to confinement, and seven times more likely to be confined than their white counterparts; Hispanics and Native Americans also receive harsher dispositions than do whites;

- race was most related to the disposition given by the court at first referral.[101]

Aside from race, research has shown a related and important factor in juvenile justice processing—socioeconomic factors. We now know that poverty, high rates of unemployment, and neighborhood disadvantages, understood as producing such dysfunctions as gambling and alcohol and drug use, are correlated to arrest, intake, adjudication, and disposition with differential outcomes that lead to confinement for those with lower socioeconomic status. Amnesty International in its 1999 report Betraying the Young[102] noted that America's juvenile justice system tends to treat children from wealthier families differently than children with lower socioeconomic status. The DMC Research Committee concurs that with wealthier children, "schools are more likely to call in parents than the police, police are more likely to call in parents than detain, and parents are more likely to retain lawyers and buy therapeutic services. The sum total of these activities is that the courts are persuaded to be more lenient than they might otherwise be towards wealthier juveniles and so contribute to class-based discrimination."[103] With such class-based discrimination, disadvantaged groups (blacks included) suffer the most because of historic inequities and systemic bias in resource distribution.

The recent report of the U. S.-based Human Rights Watch, the first state-by-state analysis of the role of race in prison sentencing, provides further evidence of the continuing resentment against American blacks.[104] The report, which focused on drugs, found glaring inequities in the rate of incarceration of African Americans compared to whites. African Americans, in ten of the thirty-seven states studied, are sent to prison on drug charges at twenty-seven to fifty times the rate for white men. Nearly 90 percent of those imprisoned on drug charges in seven other states are also African Americans. Given these disparities, Human Rights Watch recommended that repealing mandatory sentencing laws for drug offenders, increasing the availability of alternative sanctions, and eliminating racial profiling in the justice system will go a long way to address the cancer of prejudice that produces so much unfairness in our system of juvenile justice.

There is a clear sense today that race continues to impact our sense of fairness in the dispensation of justice. A few years ago, Judge Morrison England of the Federal District Court, Eastern District of California, and I were invited to speak at the Sacramento District Attorney's Citizens Academy. The Academy was organized to help bridge the gap between the Greater Sacramento community and the justice community. While I spoke about the decision points in the justice system process that are potentially susceptible to questions about fairness, Judge England spoke vigorously about the significant and unique role of the judge in that process in an increasingly multiracial and multicultural society. It is because of this unique role, he said, that judges in California were now required to undergo several days of extensive training on issues of fairness. These training sessions, which are case-driven and interactive, force judges, who like other citizens believe that they are fair, to confront issues and biases in their own lives and experiences that may, in fact, impact their own sense of fairness and the judgments that they render in the halls of justice. Other states that have not done so must draw from the lessons in California. More importantly, judicial training must include training in intercultural communication competencies. We cannot move beyond race when we have a nation with two systems of law for its own people, and when there is a culture gap between those who have been charged with dispensing justice and those who receive it.

The Mass Media

What else can we do to concretize this vision of the new dialogue of engagement in America? The mass media can play a useful role in this process. They must become educated about cultural differences and America's racial groups. They can hold town hall meetings, but such meetings must be followed with a conscious editorial policy to move away from presenting information in ways that perpetuate long-standing cultural and racial stereotypes as well as ill-feelings. Yale University political scientist Martin Gilens conducted an examination of the nation's news media in 1997 and found support for what most people already know: the media helps to perpetuate negative stereotypes about black America. For example, while most poor people in the U. S. are white as a percentage of the population, most poor people portrayed by the national news media happen to be black. Gilens' study covered a five-year period (1988–92) for three leading national magazines (Time, Newsweek, and U. S. News and World Report) and the three major television networks (ABC, NBC, and CBS). In fact, of the poor people portrayed in the magazines, 65 percent were African Americans, when data show that only 29 percent of blacks are poor. Network television news did not fare well either for the same period: 62 percent of poor people shown, for whom race could be determined, were African Americans.[105]

By consistently putting a black face on poverty, Gilens found that the American public significantly overestimates the percentage of African Americans among the nation's poor. The implications are enormous. First, in presenting information that far exceeds the reality, the mass media offer a distorted impression of the racial make-up of America's poor. Second, the inaccurate picture perpetuates long-standing negative stereotypes of the poor black person unwilling to work, and reinforces the common resentful representation of the black person in America as lazy, ignorant, and inferior. Third, the picture potentially becomes the prism through which other groups see and interact with American blacks. Ultimately, the negative portrayals harden negative attitudes towards black America, and affect the nature and quality of cross-cultural dialogue between them and the rest of America. The fact that media organizations engage in these kinds of false presentations calls into question their commitment (if any) to addressing the black problem and America's racial divide. If America is to move beyond race, there must be greater diversity and sensitivity among editors, producers, and other players who select media images for news. The sensational story, though a useful part of the capitalist media, must succumb to the more meaningful goal of telling the truth.

The White Problem

Perhaps it is important that I speak here on a point I have made in various forums: racism in America is essentially a white problem. Let me be clear about this point. First, not every white person in America is racist. Second, the province of racism is not only within the boundaries of white America. Racism is a global problem. However, in suggesting that America's racism is essentially a white problem, my goal is two-fold: first, to contextualize the discussion for the purposes of moving our nation beyond race, and second, to give the discourse on race relations in America a framework that helps our nation to find ways to root out the relics of our troubling racial history. In this context, therefore, it makes perfect sense to reason that to the extent that white Americans, as the nation's majority, set the tone for America's racial problems and challenges, they, too, given their majority and their control of the commanding heights of the nation's economy and politics, must provide the leadership needed to untangle the remaining shackles of prejudice, racism, and white supremacy in America.

In essence, the struggle to root out racism and its mate, the black problem, must not remain a black struggle only. White America must provide the leadership needed to frontally attack racism. They cannot continue to sit on the sidelines. America cannot make progress in eradicating the black problem unless white America moves. America's history demonstrates that when white America speaks and acts, change happens. If America is to move beyond race, the struggle against racism must not be the work of only the NAACP, the Urban League, black America, or brown America. It cannot be only the work of America's minorities. W. E. B. Du Bois's indictment that "The problem of the twentieth century is the problem of the color line"[106] must not remain the problem of the twenty-first century. White America must speak out, forcefully.

Regrettably, the most dismal aspect of our national dialogue on race is the near silence and the poverty of leadership on the part of white America. Leadership is the ability to direct, to guide, and to influence others towards a common cause. I remain convinced that success in our nation's dialogue on race is dependent on the quality of national leadership, in particular leadership on the part of white America. The inner guilt often felt by most of white America when matters of race are raised will not disappear until white America fully lends its voice to the struggle to defeat racism. It has a moral obligation to do so.

There is something fundamentally troubling in the psyche of individuals who make a habit of hatred or dislike of their fellow human beings merely on the basis of skin color. There is something sinister when the habit of hatred or dislike is extended to life and death issues such as the denial of access to health care and opportunities for work to feed your children, or room to house your family. And there is something more sinful when white America, through its silence, acquiesces to the habit of hatred. In 1964, Lyndon B. Johnson, a Democrat, demonstrated strong leadership when he told his party members that he was certain that their support of civil rights legislation would cost them the South. He chose the moral high road, and thus advanced black flight from the Republican Party, a party that was opposed to civil rights legislation. The picture has never been the same for Republicans, and most blacks to this day vote Democrat.

The Lott Issue

I had hoped that the Lott issue presented an historic moment for the Republican Party and for those who develop the party's platform to re-examine its message and its approach to many of the issues that shape the dialogue on race relations in America. That has not happened. And then came Hurricane Katrina, an opportunity for the dominant party in America today to show that it cared. But the opportunity was lost as the Bush administration dithered and dithered in a rather rudderless manner, as New Orleans was almost destroyed and many of its poor black citizens left to suffer by their own government. Today, many of the citizens of the carefree city commonly referred to as the Big Easy are still living as refugees in many cities in their own country. But hope is not lost yet.

First, the Republican Party must seriously begin to do something to change the prevailing perception in communities of color that the party is racist and does not care. Even President Bush acknowledged this fact in his address in July 2006 to the annual meeting of the NAACP: "I consider it a tragedy that the party of Abraham Lincoln let go its historical ties with the African American community. For too long, my party wrote off the African American vote, and many African Americans wrote off the Republican Party."[107] The party of Lincoln must not just talk about inclusion; it must act like the party of Lincoln. It must seriously engage in affirmative efforts to include persons from communities of color at the table of participation and decision-making. Words will no longer be enough.

Clearly, no political party should have a monopoly over any single ethnic group in America. Black America and other communities of color will not remain loyal to the Democrat Party if the Republican Party cleans its house. The only qualification for support by African Americans for any political party must be how best that political party addresses the black problem and advances the interests and agenda of communities of color for fairness and equity. If the Republican Party is indeed serious about building an inclusive party and reversing the negative perception that the party is racist, now is the time to show it. Putting the face of racial acceptance on the party by removing Trent Lott as its Senate majority leader will have meant nothing if there is nothing in future Republican platforms or agenda of governance to appeal to blacks and other communities of color. Now is the time to re-examine its message and approach.

Second, the Republican Party must speak out unequivocally for fairness and equity through support of legislation dealing with civil rights, voting rights, and hate crimes. They must do so with moral conviction and legitimacy. The Republican-controlled Senate and House of Representatives renewed in summer 2006 the 1965 Voting Rights Act for another twenty-five years. The Act, which ended literacy tests, poll taxes, and other devices designed to preclude blacks from voting, was a key component of the civil rights movement. It is a strange irony that more than two hundred years after the founding of our nation, black America remains the only group that has to have its ability to vote renewed. Although the Fifteenth Amendment to the U. S. Constitution barred federal or state governments from infringing on a citizen's right to vote "on account of race, color, or previous condition of servitude," that amendment had minimal impact on black ability to vote. Hence, the 1965 Voting Rights Act was passed and has now been renewed for another twenty-five years. Rather than a substantive constitutional amendment that guarantees the right to vote for all Americans, including African Americans, the Republican Congress would rather spend time on a constitutional amendment to ban gay marriage.

On affirmative action, the time has come for the party to seriously re-examine the tenability of its position that affirmative action as a national response to remedy past discrimination really constitutes racial quotas. In fact, to satisfy the views of those in the party opposed to affirmative action, Republicans have introduced the race-baiting concepts of racial quotas and reverse discrimination in the discourse. These concepts are polarizing, and do nothing to advance the discourse on what America must do to heal the lingering wounds of a historical fact—that black America and America's women were and are often still denied access to political and economic opportunities merely on the basis of their skin color or their gender.

The truth of the matter is that affirmative action emerged as a response to remedy past and continuing discrimination against blacks, then women, and then communities of color and those with disabilities. One must also recognize another truth. Affirmative action is neither a major solution to discrimination nor a sufficient means to equality. It is only one means of achieving fairness and equity. As Harvard theologian Cornell West has argued (and I agree), affirmative action is a temporary redistributive measure. It remains a crucial instrument for access and inclusion in a multiracial society, and an essential organ for reducing discrimination against women and communities of color. I agree also with West that given the history of America, "it is a virtual certainty that without affirmative action, racial and sexual discrimination would return with a vengeance. Even if affirmative action fails significantly to reduce black poverty or contributes to the persistence of racist perceptions in the workplace, without affirmative action, black access to America's prosperity would be even more difficult to obtain and racism in the workplace would persist anyway."[108]

America remains a racist society needing repair, a fact we hardly like to hear. Affirmative action has been a vital tool for access and opportunity for the most deprived segments of a society in repair—women and minorities. Affirmative action has been on the books for just thirty-five years, initially set aside for blacks who were held back for over 350 years of America's history while white America progressed. If there are problems with it, we must attack the problems, mend the program, as former President Clinton has suggested, and not end it, at least not now. Political strategist James Carville writes, "to eliminate affirmative action is to return the country to a past when jobs were controlled by whites and given mostly to whites."[109] And perhaps, as Justice Sandra Day O'Connor noted in the most recent decision of the Supreme Court on the issue, we may have no need for it twenty-five years down the road.

The irony of the argument against affirmative action is the suggestion that people hired under the program are not qualified, that skin color rather than qualification has been the most important factor. If there is any truth to this illusion, certainly part of the social responsibility for implementing an effective affirmative action program is that it should be coupled with the right kind of training and mentoring. One cannot hire any person of color simply to suggest that one was meeting affirmative action guidelines, but then ignore the equally important need to provide the necessary and sufficient conditions for success. Real commitment to racial healing must be coupled with real commitment to the philosophy of inclusion. One aspect of the complaints from black America and communities of color is that employers hire and set them up for failure. The result becomes "I told you so," "I knew he would not do well"—a self-fulfilling prophesy, which lends weight to the false argument that affirmative action encourages mediocrity. Nothing could be further from the truth.

Yet some in black America, especially conservative black intellectuals and among them those whom I describe as the nouveaux elites (the new elites), have fallen prey to the unfortunate misconception that racism is not a barrier, or that their black brethren may not, in fact, be qualified for the access and opportunities provided through affirmative action. The nouveaux elites represent new kinds of conservative black intellectuals, politicians, businessmen and women, as well as entertainers, with humble beginnings or modest backgrounds, whose new-found personal success and individual achievement have caused them to turn their backs on the collective experience of their people, choosing instead to become the official apologists for the conservative agenda. Among them are Supreme Court Associate Justice Clarence Thomas, former Congressman J. C. Watts, former University of California regent Ward Connerly, Berkeley linguist John McWhorter, radio talk-show host Armstrong Williams, and scholar Shelby Steele.

The resentment towards affirmative action, as if the playing field were now equal, among this class of nouveaux elites is perhaps in part a response to white perception about their own qualifications. It seems to me that one way, in their view, that America can end racism, or that black America can end the perception in white America that they may not be qualified for the access and opportunities secured under affirmative action guidelines, is to end the redistributive principles enshrined in affirmative action, and to return America to a pre-affirmative-action status quo. They are wrong. If we are to move beyond race, Americans—black and white, brown, red, and yellow, men and women, young and old, straight and gay—must speak with one voice in confronting all forms of resentment that seek to keep one group down and the other up. We must confront xenophobia and hatred of all kinds for the sake of our union and our democracy.

ON DAVID HOROWITZ AND HIS CASE AGAINST REPARATIONS

At this place, liberty and life were stolen and sold. Human beings were delivered and sorted and weighed and branded with the marks of commercial enterprises and loaded as cargo on a voyage without return … One of the largest migrations of history was also one of the greatest crimes of history.

President George W. Bush

African Americans had answered the country's every call from its infancy … Yet, the fame and fortune that were their just due never came. For their blood spent, lives lost, and battles won, they received nothing. They went back to slavery, real or economic, consigned there by hate, prejudice, bigotry, and intolerance.

Colin Powell

One cannot object to the idea of the concept of compensation to individuals for wrongs which they have suffered. There is certainly no wrong more grievous, after the wronged loss of life, than the loss of liberty.

Lord Wilberforce

Reparation is not the money the campaign may or may not bring: the most important part of reparation is our self-repair; the change it will bring about in our understanding of our history, of ourselves, and our destiny; the change it will bring about in our place in the world … For the sad truth is that five centuries of holocaust have made our societies brittle and unviable.

Chinweizu

On David Horowitz's Case against Reparations

The advertisement[110] by David Horowitz entitled "Ten Reasons Why Reparations for Slavery Is a Bad Idea. And Racist Too" once again thrust the issue of race into the forefront of our national dialogue. The paid advertisement, seen by some as very disturbing, was sent to student newspapers of some at the nation's major centers of intellectual pursuits, including the Daily Cal of the University of California, Berkeley and the California Aggie at the University of California, Davis. Both newspapers published the advertisement, but then retracted the publication when the local black community protested.

The content of the advertisement is especially engaging and worth revisiting because it speaks to the continuing challenge posed by race in building an American community. Among Horowitz's arguments are that "there is no single group responsible for the crime of slavery," that "there is no one group that benefited from its fruits," and "only a tiny minority of white Americans ever owned slaves."[111] Furthermore, he argued that "reparations to African Americans have already been paid in the form of welfare and racial preferences" and that "the reparations claim is a separatist idea that sets African Americans against the nation that gave them freedom." Those are pretty strong words.

Horowitz's ad is particularly daring because he said in public what many today in white America have been feeling and saying quietly in their bedrooms: we are not responsible for the crime of slavery; we have made too many concessions already; the idea of reparations is unworkable and impractical. It is very divisive. And we need to move on.

If America is to move on, it must confront now what is shaping up as one of the major racial challenges of the twenty-first century. The problems with Horowitz's argument are multi-fold. First, the contention that no single group is responsible for the crime of slavery has no validity. Yes, it is no secret that continental Africans participated in the crime of slavery. While one must admit the wrongness of African participation in the crime of slavery, global history is littered with stories of individuals who turned against their own people. History is also littered with stories of individuals who were used by the "enemies" for their own personal greed and aggrandizement. In truth, however, the single driving force in Africa's complicity in the crime of slavery was Europe and white America. The purposeful journey to Africa for human capital was carefully hatched in Europe and white America by Europe and white America. The mass capture of Africans was carefully executed in Africa by Europe and white America, of course, with local connivance, where the help of individual Africans became necessary. The unimaginable horrors of the Middle Passage powerfully recreated in Steven Spielberg's movie Amistad, in which millions of Africans lost their lives on the high seas, was witnessed by Europe and white America.

In his authoritative book A People's History of the United States, Howard Zinn writes, "The conditions of capture and sale were crushing … The marches to the coast, sometimes for 1000 miles, with people shackled around the neck, under whip and gun, were death marches, in which two of every five blacks died. On the coast, they were kept in cages until they were picked and sold."[112]

Other accounts have noted that those who were considered sound and good for the voyage to the New World were branded on the breast with a red-hot iron, imprinting the mark of the Dutch, English, and French companies who owned the captured Africans. Usually two weeks after capture, the branded slaves were shipped to their destinations—on the plantations of Europe and North America. All serious accounts of the history of the slave trade show unquestionably that the chattelisation of those Africans who made it to Europe and the Americas was a project of Europe and white America. The decimation of the languages and cultures that the Africans brought with them to Europe and the New World was also a part of the international project on slavery. Clearly the major responsibility, if one is honest, for the crime of slavery rests squarely at the doorsteps of Europe and white America. Certainly one cannot ignore the role of some individuals in the Arab world in the trans-Saharan slave trade, in which millions of Africans also lost their lives. Arab merchants also bear some responsibility. As the historian Chancellor Williams writes, "Blacks are in Arabia for precisely the same reasons Blacks are in the U. S., South America, and the Caribbean Islands—through capture and enslavement."[113]

I commend Horowitz for at least accepting that slavery was a crime. Horowitz is also right in suggesting that "no one single group is responsible for the crime" of slavery. Clearly Europe and the Arab world were involved in the enslavement of African people, but by focusing on the argument that "no one single group is responsible for the crime," he minimizes the enormous benefits reaped by Americans of European ancestry in one of the worst crimes against humanity in recorded history. After all, the trans-Atlantic slave trade, which involved Europe and white America, helped to finance (through free labor) the industrial revolution. We cannot move beyond race until America officially acknowledges the crime of slavery and offers a sincere apology.

Certainly I am not suggesting that individuals should feel any guilt for atrocities that occurred in 1840, that they did not approve of, and that may have been resisted—even to the point of death—by their own ancestors. But since white America still benefits economically from what happened a century ago, an official apology that acknowledges the crime of slavery represents an important first step toward cultural unity.

African Slavery

It has been argued that slavery existed in Africa for centuries before outsiders began to engage in the trade. This is true. But the scope, character, and substance of slavery in Africa were not the same as the trans-Atlantic slave trade. Many of those who served as slaves before the coming of Europeans were captured during times of war. As bounties of war, they were made to serve in the king's court, or as the elders of the community would deem fit. They were not bought, they were not regarded as less human, and they were not subjected to cruel and unusual punishment. They had their dignity. They retained their languages, culture, and humanity. In sum, they had rights and responsibilities which American and European slavery did not and could not permit. Howard Zinn writes that "African slavery lacked two elements that made American slavery the most cruel form of slavery in history: The frenzy for limitless profit that comes from capitalistic agriculture; the reduction of the slave to less than human status by the use of racial hatred, with that relentless clarity based on color, where white was master, black was slave."[114]

Certainly, one cannot compare African slavery to the harsh conditions of service on the cotton plantations of North America where the depravation of freedom reigned supreme, and where also the loss of their African names, identity, language, ethnic and family structures, and other constitutive elements of African culture was the principal instrument for the success of slavery. Overall, the slave trade across the Atlantic was morally and culturally devastating as well as destructive of family bonds. Its goal was the consignment of Africans to a life of endless servitude in America. One cannot draw any comparison in this regard to the forms of slavery that existed in Africa before European arrival.

It has also been argued that far more people were enslaved internally in Africa than were ever exported across the Atlantic. This is not true. No one knows exactly how many Africans were stolen from their homes. No one knows exactly how many died in the struggles to resist the new enemies. But various estimates have suggested that some ten to one hundred million Africans were kidnapped and sold to plantation owners in the New World. Millions more perished during the journey. Randall Robinson suggests "anywhere from ten to twenty-five million Africans died in slave ships en route from Africa to the Americas."[115] Howard Zinn writes, "Africa lost 50 million human beings to death and slavery in those centuries we call the beginnings of modern Western civilization, at the hands of slave traders and plantation owners in Western Europe and America, the countries deemed the most advanced in the world."[116] There is no respected scholarly evidence or authority I know of that indicates that far more people were internally enslaved on the continent of Africa. If there is any truth to the claim, one is then compelled to ask what became of these so-called slaves in Africa when slavery ended in both Europe and the Americas? Where are their descendants? And how long did the internal slavery in Africa last? Any argument that minimizes the crime of slavery—whether it was slavery in Africa, in Europe, or in the New World—through a process of quantification is both misleading and intellectually dishonest. Whether the number is small or large does nothing to minimize the crime of slavery.

Slavery in Europe and the Americas

We know that the Dutch first dominated the slave trade. The English later joined and were followed by Americans. Participation in the slave trade was essentially confined to individual traders and companies. Any active participation from the governments of Western nations was minimal. But slavery could not have survived or lasted as long as it did on its own. It was an institution sanctioned by Western governments as well as the church. In the end, the work of the abolitionist movement and the recognition of the horrendous cruelty of this enterprise by the government of the United Kingdom led to the abolition of slavery in Britain in 1807, and in all of the British colonies between 1834 and 1840. On January 1, 1863, President Abraham Lincoln signed the Emancipation Proclamation abolishing slavery in the U. S. By 1885, slavery was abolished in Latin America. Clearly the states had the authority to end slavery, but lacked the moral courage to do so. It is no secret that many of the political leaders of the time owned slaves themselves. Among them were Lincoln and Jefferson.

We know that the abolition of slavery in the U. S. in 1863 did not come with equal citizenship rights for African Americans. American blacks could not drink from the same water fountains as whites. American blacks could not sit at the same lunch counters. American blacks could only sit in the back when they went to movie theaters. American blacks could not be hired for certain positions. Access to various opportunities open to white Americans, was denied. The right to vote did not come until the ratification of the Fifteenth Amendment to the Constitution in1870 following the Civil War. The Fifteenth Amendment barred federal or state governments from infringing on a citizen's right to vote "on account of race, color, or previous condition of servitude." Even so, for nearly a century, the ratification of the Fifteenth Amendment had little impact on black voting rights. In the South, various devices—from terrorism to the poll tax, literacy tests and grandfather clauses—were employed to keep blacks from voting. Various Congressional actions and Supreme Court rulings eventually struck down voting restrictions across the country, especially in the South. In 1965, Congress passed the Voting Rights Act to increase black voter registration by empowering the Justice Department to closely monitor voting processes and discrimination across the country. What happened during the 2000 elections in Florida, in which many blacks were denied the right to vote or had their votes not counted after they were cast, continues to raise questions about America's commitment to ensuring that its black citizens fully enjoy the rights enjoyed by all Americans.

Martin Luther King, Jr. noted that "virtually all of the Founding Fathers of our nation, even those who rose to the heights of the Presidency, those whom we cherish as our authentic heroes, were so enmeshed in the ethos of slavery and white supremacy that not one ever emerged with a clear, unambiguous stand on Negro rights."[117] We face the same situation today on reparations. Virtually all of our nation's leaders, even those who have risen to the heights of the Presidency, Senators, members of the House of Representatives, those we cherish as authentic heroes and leaders of substance, not one except those in the Congressional Black Caucus has ever emerged with a clear, unambiguous stand on reparations for black America. It is possible then to argue that like most of white America, they share Horowitz's position.

Existing evidence does not support Horowitz's arguments that there is no one group that benefited from the fruits of slavery and that "only a tiny minority of white Americans ever owned slaves." One of the reasons slavery was so difficult to root out was that it had become institutional—a way of life and a means of economic empowerment for so many, and a veritable source of cheap labor for both the private and public sectors of our society. There were many whites in the powerful abolitionist movement who risked their lives to end it. There were many whites who became poor after the Civil War and may not have benefited directly from slavery. However, reasonable people on both sides of the issue would agree that while some whites may not have benefited financially from slavery, one cannot ignore the massive loss suffered by those put into slavery, who according to President Bush "entered a society indifferent to their anguish and made prosperous by their unpaid labor."[118] In remarks made in East Africa at the Kisowera Community School in Mukono, Uganda, in 1998, President

Clinton noted that "going back to the time before we were even a nation, European Americans received the fruits of the slave trade. And we were wrong in that."[119] In making those remarks, Clinton did acknowledge white America's enrichment from the fruits of slavery, and in fact became the only U. S. president to have come close on the question of apology for slavery. "We were wrong on that," he said, but unfortunately he offered no plans for righting the wrongs of slavery.

A few years ago, in a telephone conversation I had with Ali Mazrui, a member of the Eminent Persons Group appointed by the Organization of African Unity (OAU) to explore the issue of African Reparations for Enslavement and Colonization, I was reminded that Clinton's admission of regret, although not a full apology, reflected a changing political climate conducive for a new dialogue on reparations, not only in the U. S., but also in the African Diaspora. Without recognition, he argued, of the growing African American role and presence in the U. S. political and economic landscape, it would have been inconceivable that a U. S. president would come so close to offering a formal apology for slavery.

Generations of white Americans, like Horowitz, have insisted that they were not part of the problem; that they did not create or participate in slavery; and that only a tiny fraction of white Americans owned slaves. There is no question that the successors of those who instigated slavery were from white America; the successors of those who conducted the trade in human cargo were also from white America; those who profited tremendously from it also came from white America. Prominent historians and social scientists who have written at length on the subject all agree that African Americans, who remain victims of one of the most extensive criminal projects in human history, still suffer from the debilitating effects of the crime.

Is Reparations a Racist Idea?

I turn now to address a very important question: is the idea of reparations a racist one? Horowitz's ad is entitled "Ten Reasons Why Reparations is a Bad Idea. And Racist Too." Any charge that reparations is racist is very interesting, but completely illogical.

Racism derives from the idea that people are different and that one racial group is superior to the other. The defining characteristics that constitute the difference are physical traits such as skin color, facial structure, hair color and texture, and eye shape. In this sense, persons or groups who perceive themselves as superior based on these characteristics place less value on the beliefs, values, and norms of the group they perceive as inferior. Racism thrives within the context of power and control, including the power to oppress and exploit. Those who have the power and the control invariably exercise them in the allocation or exploitation of resources in ways that systematically favor persons from their own racial group at the expense of others. Those who make the decisions about who gets hired, who gets the promotion, who gets to have an office with a window, who gets to have a computer, who gets to attend special training, and so on, are all open to charges of racism, depending on how they exercise the power and the authority. Decisions on issues related to access to social, political, and economic power are also open to charges of racism.

Racism is fundamentally exclusionary because it strives to keep certain people (based on certain physical qualities) from equal participation in society's institutions. Scholars agree that "racism is the tendency by groups in control of institutional and cultural power to use it to keep members of groups who do not have access to the same kinds of power at a disadvantage."[120] The cumulative effect of racism over time, write scholars Phyllis Katz and Dalmas Taylor,[121] is the oppression and exploitation of ethnic minorities who, because of circumstances of history, lack the power and the control over resource allocation. The circumstances of history have been the context in which slavery operated—causing enormous harm to its victims for which full restitution is clearly essential. To suggest that victims of slavery—those who are seeking redress from long years of racist conduct that deprived them of their liberty—are now racist, is, to say the least, specious. And even as I write, more work is needed to alter the structures of power and control that continue to bear witness to the cumulative legacies of slavery.

Black-White Perceptions of Racism

It is quite possible to fall into the thinking trap that an idea that attempts to correct wrong-doing created by a racist philosophy is also racist. This trap is possibly where Horowitz stands his case. But his charge raises a more important and profound question: how do white America and black America perceive racism? Most whites see racist behaviors embedded in "individual acts of meanness." Most blacks and persons of color see racism embedded in institutional frameworks. Let us explore these ideas further.

"I was taught to see racism only in individual acts of meanness, not in invisible systems conferring dominance on my group,"[122] writes Peggy McIntosh, a white woman whose work has influenced generations of thought on racism and white privilege. In seeing racism in "individual acts of meanness," most whites accept that any person is capable of being racist. This perception and definition of racism is important but only partially correct, essentially because in the U. S. context, it ignores "invisible systems" (and I might add visible systems) conferring from birth unsought racial preferences, advantages, and dominance on persons of European background. This has been the fact of American social life. Black perception of racism draws from this perspective. Black America sees racism and racist behaviors as existing not in individual acts of meanness, but in "the way society as a whole is arranged, and how the economic, education, cultural and social rewards of that society are distributed."[123] The institutional framework perspective suggests that those who have power and control over society's institutional and cultural systems (the invisible and visible systems), and the privilege to decide how rewards are distributed within society's systems (regardless of location), have the capacity for racist conduct. Black argument (also accepted by other racial minority groups) about racism stands on this reasoning. This explanation may be hard for white America to deal with, for those (in particular white males) who have historically had the power and control over allocation of resources in the U. S. In this light the case for—or against—reparations must be understood.

Privilege in White America

In 1988, Peggy McIntosh of the Center for Research on Women at Wellesley College, Wellesley, Massachusetts, wrote a fascinating and telling piece about the privilege that white America has, but almost always denies. The piece (which includes a list of male privileges) is worth quoting:

> Thinking through unacknowledged male privilege as a phenomenon, I realized that, since hierarchies in our society are interlocking, there was most likely a phenomenon of white privilege that was similarly denied and protected. As a white person, I realized I had been taught about racism as something that puts others at a disadvantage, but had not been taught not to see one of its corollary aspects, white privilege, which puts me at an advantage. I think whites are carefully taught not to recognize white privilege, as males are taught not to recognize male privilege. So I have begun in an untutored way to ask what it is like to have white privilege. I have come to see white privilege as an invisible package of unearned assets that I can count on cashing in each day, but about which I was "meant" to remain oblivious.
>
> White privilege is like an invisible weightless knapsack of special provisions, maps, passports, codebooks, visas, clothes, tools, and bank checks. Describing white privilege makes one newly accountable. As we in women's studies work to reveal male privilege, and ask men to give up some of their power, so one who writes about having white privilege must ask, "having described it, what will I do to lesson or end it?"[124]

In this piece, McIntosh identifies more than forty areas of privilege and advantage enjoyed by white America over other groups, noting that "most talk by whites about equal opportunity seems ... now to be about equal opportunity to try to get into a position of dominance while denying that systems of dominance exist ... Obliviousness about white advantage, like obliviousness about male advantage, is kept strongly inculturated in the

U. S. so as to maintain the myth of meritocracy, the myth that democratic choice is equally available to all."[125] But choice, as reasonable Americans would admit, is not equally available to all Americans. The same can be said of power and privilege.

Understanding Privilege and Power

Power accords a certain privilege. Most people who have privilege accorded to them because they are part of a majority population are unaware of such privilege. Consider the following example, which I have shared with students enrolled in my intercultural communication courses at the university. During the first week of classes, I typically ask my students to tell me if they noticed any difference in how the seats in the classroom are configured. Most students would look around the classroom, and almost always would tell me that they do not see any difference, or that they do not know, and have not paid attention. The point of the question is to draw their attention to a simple yet inescapable element of diversity in their classroom and how power and privilege are implicated in a multicultural and multiracial society—the presence of right-handed chairs for students who are right-handed, and then left-handed chairs for students who are left-handed. At California State University, Sacramento, where I taught for many years, the chairs in the classrooms are logically color-coded. The red chairs are for students who are left-handed, and the blue ones are for students who are right-handed. The majority of the chairs are generally coded in blue, because most students are right-handed. Cal State, Sacramento recognizes the presence of left-handed students on its campus, and takes the extra step to ensure that the left-handed students are comfortable in the classroom when they come for lectures—by giving them the same privilege that the right-handed majority enjoys. While the minority students (left-handed students) notice the difference in the chairs, the majority students (right-handed) do not. Everything is the same for them. It is amazing to watch how they walk through the class; they enjoy the privilege, without knowing that they do. For them, the privilege is almost invisible. The system or the institution has always been set up to benefit them. While they are aware that some of their classmates may be left-handed, that awareness is the extent of their knowledge. They are shocked then when their attention is drawn to the privilege they have enjoyed all this time. Clearly, those who make the decisions about what type of chairs to get are typically right-handed.

Using the same logic, I present a scenario in which I ask the students to respond to hypothetical situations in which left-handed students begin an agitation for more left-handed chairs at the university. Some of the right-handed students respond that their first instinct will be to resist the request, because of the concern that left-handed students may begin to ask for more. "We just don't have the resources to get them what they want," one student remarked. Another commented, "If we get them the chairs, they are going to ask for something else." Several other phrases came from my students: "We have given them this; we have made concessions, yet they want more." It was amazing to listen to these students, and I took note of the constant expression "we" that permeated all of their remarks. When right-handed people do eventually provide the chairs, they see themselves as "helping them," of doing a benevolent service, rather than performing an act that allows for equity in outcomes, that opens the same doors of opportunity and access they, as right-handed students, continue to enjoy. Students who are left-handed of course are understandably angry at the generally condescending tone of the right-handed students.

The color-coded chair exercise is illuminating, because it underscores the challenges of the discourse on the fairness of the modus operandi for resource allocation in a diverse society. Right-handed students, like most whites, have come to "think of their lives as morally neutral, normative, and average, and also ideal, so that when 'they' work to benefit others, this is seen as work which will allow 'them' to be more like 'us.'"[126] When white America works to benefit minority groups, it is almost always seen as work which will allow them to be more like "us." This has been the state of America's union. White America does not see such work as essential to equalizing the playing field and to ensuring equity in outcomes. Minority groups who do not have the privilege ultimately see their struggle as one designed to equalize the playing field. Unfortunately, those who have the privilege deny that they have it, or sometimes unconsciously do not recognize the existence of such privilege. Thus ignorance about white privilege permeates white America today. Any effort to equalize the field is painted as reverse discrimination.

When Horowitz, who is white-skinned, describes the quest for reparations by African Americans as racist, he, like right-handed people, or males, denies or is not aware of the privilege his whiteness has accorded him all his life, and he exposes himself to the charge that he might be racist. Like Horowitz, many white Americans are unaware that some of their actions and behaviors expose a racist attitude (a mindset) invisible to themselves, but clear from their actions and behaviors to those who are victims of the attitude. This is why racism is such a complicated subject. How could a group that has experienced centuries of oppression and exploitation solely on the basis of their physical properties be said to be racist in an arena in which they have had no power and control? Racism is not just about individual acts of meanness. Racism is the tendency by groups in control of institutional and cultural power to use such power to keep other groups (intentionally or unintentionally) at a disadvantage or to deny them access to resources. Arguments for reparations would not be necessary if black Americans had power and control, or if they shared them with white Americans. Put simply, there would be no need for reparations if massive and unconscionable exploitation and deprivation had not occurred. This historical fact drives the growing movement for restitution.

The On-Again, Off-Again Support for Civil Rights

Horowitz's ad cannot be simply dismissed or ignored. Placed in its proper context, it speaks to a fundamental moral crisis in American society—the on-again, off-again support for civil rights. In one moment, most white Americans are for civil rights; in another moment, they are unsure where they stand, and many on the left continue to assume they are doing minorities a favor. It is a sad place for a nation in search of justice to be.

In the past fifteen years in particular, we have witnessed a variety of assaults on civil rights issues. Assault on civil rights is certainly not new. What is new today is the rise of a new crop of prominent conservative intellectuals, especially white conservatives, joined now by a few black conservatives, relentlessly bent on dismantling the civil rights project. Surely, those on the conservative right must find some succor that they too have support even from many on America's left who have been conspicuously silent on the question of reparations. If America is to move beyond race and build a genuine community, civil rights must be seen not as white privilege or black rights but as basic human rights. And the quest for reparations represents a just cause for unjust acts committed against a racial group. How long ago the acts occurred does not diminish the acts or their impact.

Why Reparations Are Important

Reparation remains an essential pillar to black empowerment and economic development. In his book The Debt: What America Owes Black America, Randall Robinson makes the profound case that America cannot move beyond race unless it confronts the issue of reparations. Writes Robinson, "Solutions must be tailored to the scope of the crime in a way that would make the victim whole. In this case, the psychic and economic injury is enormous, multidimensional and long-running. Thus must be America's restitution to blacks for the damage done."[127] Serious commitments to correct past wrongs and injuries, not half measures, are needed to move our nation beyond race.

Even when viewed in a global context, the quest for reparations is certainly not new. Beyond the moral argument, there is a legal basis for it that is well recognized in U. S. jurisprudence as well as in international law. The law recognizes that restitution is a legitimate means of offering compensation to an injured party. U. S. courts have long accepted the idea of payment of compensation or damages to an injured party by the party which caused the harm. In 1928, in a case involving Germany and Poland, the International Court of Justice ruled that those who commit crimes against humanity must make reparation:

> The essential principle contained in the actual notion of an illegal act—a
> principle which seems to be established by international practice and in

particular by the decisions of arbitral tribunals—is that reparation must, as far as possible, wipe out all the consequences of the illegal act and re-establish the situation which would, in all probability, have existed if that act had not been committed. Restitution in kind or, if this is not possible, payment of a sum corresponding to the value which a restitution in kind would bear; the reward, if need be, of damages for loss sustained which would not be covered by restitution in kind or payment in place of it— such are the principles which should serve to determine the amount of compensation due for an act contrary to international law.[128]

Precedence for Reparations

Beyond this legal basis, there is established precedence on the quest for reparations. We know of reparation claims in Europe, Asia, South America, and North America. For example, it is no secret that West Germany paid reparations to the state of Israel for the crimes of the Nazi Holocaust. Lord Anthony Gifford, one of the leading proponents of restitution, has noted that Germany's reparations to Israel were made "even though the state of Israel did not exist at the time when the Nazi regime committed its crimes against the Jews. It is also significant that West Germany, which felt obliged to meet the claim, was also a different state, territorially as well as politically, from the German Reich, which was responsible for the atrocities."[129] This position is important because it acknowledges that a country's existence is generally continuous, and that acts supported by the state must be accounted for regardless of whether that government has ceased to exist or whether the particular act, i.e., slavery or genocide, for which the state is faulted, is no longer tenable or defensible. New governmental arrangements do not exculpate or exonerate the state from responsibility or culpability. Thus the argument about who did what and when in Horowitz's case against reparations for black America fails to meet the test of legal validity. Some may argue that West Germany did not send soldiers to fight and die to save the Jews. That is true. Some would also argue that white America did fight and die to free slaves. That too is true. Without minimizing the white role in freeing American blacks from slavery, it is important to note that what happens after freedom is gained is as important as the freedom itself.

The initial phase of German reparations to Jews included separate payments for various purposes amounting to several billion dollars. Payments have gone directly to victims as personal indemnities and to inmates of the concentration camps for the period they were incarcerated. Payments have also been made to the Israeli government for the resettlement of thousands of Jewish émigrés from territories formerly under Hitler's control; and pension payments have gone to survivors of the victims of the Nazi holocaust. As recently as 1992, the New York-based World Jewish Congress announced that the newly-unified Germany would make reparations totaling $63 million to another set of 50,000 Jews who had suffered Nazi persecution. This group, which had lived in East Germany while it was still a separate communist state, could not receive reparations because of their place of residence.[130]

Lessons from Germany and other Places

There are some lessons to be learned by America from German and Jewish leaders on the spirit and the modalities they have employed in reaching the various agreements and arrangements for restitution for victims of the Jewish Holocaust. There is no way Germany, as a society, would have moved beyond the Holocaust, or beyond the blame, without full restitution for the crimes of Nazi Germany, including an official apology and an acceptance of responsibility. If America is to move beyond race, it should apply the same moral principle as Germany on the vexing issue of slavery—an official apology and acceptance of responsibility. The time to heal is now.

At the end of World War II, the Allied powers also demanded reparations totaling $320 million from Germany for all atrocities committed during the war. The atrocities for which reparations claims were made included loss of life, loss of liberty, loss of property, disorganization of family, and forced relocation to concentration camps on the basis of racial, religious, and political affiliations. Italy and Finland also paid reparations. In Asia, Japan paid reparations totaling more than $39 million to countries it occupied during World War II. And North Korea, which has received an official apology from the Japanese Government, has asked for $5 billion in reparations for damages it incurred during thirty-five years of Japanese occupation and colonization.

In the Americas, there are reparation claims in Chile (involving the Mapuche people), in Canada (involving the Eskimo), and in the U. S. (involving the Sioux, Navaho, and Hopi Indian nations). All claims are for restitution of ancestral lands forcibly taken by European immigrants. In 1988, the U. S. government admitted that its internment of Americans of Japanese ancestry during World War II was wrong, and the government proceeded to pay reparations of $20,000 to each internee, for a total of $1.2 billion. This was a bold move, and Americans understood it. The absence of the same bold move on the issue of reparations for American blacks deprived of the same basic freedoms and more for centuries remains puzzling.

As recently as 1995, Queen Elizabeth II of the United Kingdom offered an official apology to the Maori people of New Zealand for crimes committed against them by British settlers in 1863, and she personally signed the Royal Assent to the Waikato Raupatu Claims Settlement Bill. The bill allowed the government of New Zealand to pay reparations for lands seized from the Maoris by British settlers. (The Queen is New Zealand's head of state.) More recently, we have a reparations claim from the government of Kuwait over alleged atrocities committed by Iraq following its 1991 invasion of the tiny kingdom.

While no reparations claim can fully compensate for the loss of life and liberty, clearly the precedent for it exists. People of African descent are merely latecomers to the scene. Those who have exercised their right to make such claim for reparations as permitted under U. S. jurisprudence and international law have never been accused of being racist. Horowitz's argument that the demand for reparations by black America is racist defies logic. When other groups ask, it is not racist, but when blacks ask, it becomes a racist idea.

Horowitz's other claim, that "reparations to African Americans have already been paid … in the form of welfare and racial preferences," is ridiculous. Prior to the passage of the 1994 Welfare Reform Bill, there always were more whites (in terms of sheer numbers) on welfare rolls than any other group. With less education, lower incomes, and more children, blacks and other groups are finding it harder to exit the welfare rolls, leaving some experts to conclude that the "growing minority share of the rolls could erode support for welfare spending and reinforce racial bias in general."[131] The fundamental question remains: If welfare payments to black America constitute reparations for crimes of slavery, how does one justify the same payments to white recipients, who have been on the rolls, and have not been victims of the crime of slavery? The argument about racial preferences falls flat when subjected to scrutiny. No single group in American society has benefited more from racial preferences than white America.

I turn now to one more argument in Horowitz's ad: "the reparations claim is a separatist idea that sets African Americans against the nation that gave them freedom." There can be nothing more insulting, more condescending, and more egotistical than this charge. It ignores the historical context of how Africans were robbed of the very freedom that Horowitz claims the nation gave them. It also ignores the nature of the freedom that the nation gave to African Americans in 1863. What happened to the government promise to former slaves of "forty acres and a mule" at the end of slavery? What happened to so-called freed slaves who spoke out and were arrested on charges of sedition? What happened to the right to vote granted after the Civil War under the Fifteenth Amendment to the U. S. Constitution, because the so-called right lacked any enforcement mechanism for fully permitting blacks to participate in America's democratic process?

Martin Luther King, Jr. noted that the liberation from slavery in 1863 meant a formal legal freedom in which four million black people in the South owned their skins and nothing more. In his words,

> With civil war still dividing the nation, a new inferno engulfed the Negro and his family. Thrown off the plantations, penniless, homeless, still largely

in the territory of their enemies and in the grip of fear, bewilderment and aimlessness, hundreds of thousands became wanderers. For security they fled to Union Army camps that were unprepared to help. One writer describes a mother carrying a child in one arm, a father holding another child, and eight children with their hands tied to one rope held by the mother, [they] traveled hundreds of miles to safety. All were not so fortunate. In the starvation-induced madness some Negroes killed their children to free them of their misery.[132]

Historical accounts, according to King, further indicate that after the Civil War, millions of blacks returned to a new form of slavery, once again

imprisoned on plantations devoid of human rights and plunged into searing poverty generation after generation. Some families found their way to the North, in a movement E. Franklin Frazier aptly describes as "into the city of destruction." Illiterate, afraid and crushed by want, they were herded into the slums. The bewildering complexity of the city undermined the confidence of fathers and mothers, causing them to lose control of their children, whose bewilderment was even more acute ... Because the institution of marriage had been illegal under slavery, and because of indiscriminate sex relations, often with their white masters, mothers could identify their children but frequently not their children's fathers. Moreover, the women, being more generally in the house and charged with the care of the white master's children, were more often exposed to some education and a sense—though minimal—of personal worth. Hence a matriarchy had early developed. After slavery it persisted because in the cities there was more employment for women than for men. Though both were unskilled, the women could be used in domestic service at low wages. The woman became the support of the household and the matriarchy was reinforced. The Negro male existed in a larger society dominated by men, but he was subordinated to women in his own society. ... The quest of the Negro male for employment was always frustrating. If he lacked skill, he was only occasionally wanted because such employment as he could find had little regularity and even less remuneration. If he had a skill, he also had his black skin, and discrimination locked doors against him. In the competition for scarce jobs he was a loser because he was born that way.[133]

So much for Horowitz's and America's freedom to black America: formal, empty, unenforceable, and meaningless. Blacks owned their skin and nothing more. In essence, in spite of the emancipation claim, white America progressed further, while black America's hands were tied through the invisible and visible structures of the time that encouraged and promoted discrimination on the basis of skin color. It took more than one hundred years after slavery was abolished for Congress to pass the 1964 Voting Rights Act that gave teeth to the U. S. Justice Department to enforce the letter and the spirit of the Fifteenth Amendment. And each day, an attempt is made by Horowitz and company to chip away at the very same freedom.

Steps We Must Take

What can be done? A five-point agenda is provided here to guide the discourse on restitution.

1. America must recognize and accept that the campaign for reparations by black America is morally just and legal, and that there are precedents for it. Slavery remains America's oldest wound, creating emotions that divide and sometimes tear the nation apart. Thus, strong leadership is called for, requiring an official acknowledgement of the wrongs of slavery and an apology. We cannot close this wound unless America takes the authentic step toward genuine healing by first offering an official apology for the wrongs of slavery.

2. Congress can no longer look the other way. It has been more than a decade since Congressman John Conyers, a Democrat from Michigan, introduced a bill in Congress to establish a commission to study the matter and to make recommendations on appropriate remedies. Nothing substantive has happened to that bill since 1993. As the "peoples' house," Congress must begin the process of identifying meaningful strategies to address the lingering effects of slavery in the same way it provided leadership on reparations for the victims of the Japanese internment camps in the U. S.

3. It is time for presidential leadership on the issue. In this context, a presidential commission on African American reparations is urgently needed. In 1979, President Carter established the Presidential Commission on the Holocaust. The work of that commission led to the creation of a Permanent National Memorial on the Holocaust and a renewed commitment to prevent genocide. It is time for the White House and the president to establish a presidential commission on African American reparations. The commission's task would be to explore the modalities for German-Jewish amity on the subject and make recommendations on how America might proceed. A few years ago, African heads of states and governments appointed an Eminent Persons Group on African Reparations for Enslavement and Colonization, chaired by the late Chief Moshood Abiola of Nigeria, (the presumed winner of the 1992 presidential elections), to explore the issue. The group identified four major issues in the African demand that are worth citing here:

   • capital transfer in the form of the Marshall Plan, designed in the 1940s to bring Europe out of the quagmires of World War II. In this case, the proposal for capital transfer to Africa is aimed at providing financial capacity essential for reconstruction and development to pull Africa out of the lingering effects of enslavement and colonization;

- skills transfer in the form of building the indigenous capacity to deal with economic development in such areas as education, agriculture, and so forth;

- power-sharing arrangements so as to provide Africa with greater say in such global institutions as the United Nations Security Council, the World Bank, and the International Monetary Fund; and

- resources transfer in the form of economic support to Pan African groups from various governments and multilateral agencies that have benefited in the past and continue to benefit now from Africa's abundant resources.[134]

The presidential commission on African American reparations should study the content of OAU Eminent Persons Group to see what can be learned from it, especially because of its relationship to the reparations demand in the U. S.

4. Investment in America's future through a twenty-five-year educational investment fund in black America. The fund would provide free universal access to education for all African Americans, and would represent the nation's serious commitment to the massive uplifting of black people from the despair of poverty. Education remains a principal tool for lifting people out of poverty and preparing them for meeting the challenges of the present and the future. It is also one of the best defenses against racism. Given the current state of social and economic dislocation in black America today, education remains a vitally needed enterprise for integrating blacks in today's fast-moving knowledge economy.

5. Proponents of the reparations claim must intensify the campaign for reparations for black America. If history tells us anything, it is that each piece of freedom attained by black America has come only with a struggle. America has never given freedom to blacks on a platter. Opposition to the struggle at international fora or on the home front should not be seen as a surprise, and should not deter proponents from what is precisely a moral and just cause. We must be reminded that well-meaning Americans opposed the abolition of slavery, and many opposed the civil rights movement and the passage of subsequent legislation under President Johnson. In the end, common sense prevailed. No matter how long it may take, common sense will prevail in the just struggle to find a common center on the issue of restitution. Here the civil rights community must fashion an agenda and a strategy for pursuing the agenda.

In sum, I must underscore an important point made earlier. There is need to explore the modalities for reparations employed in other similar claims for reparations. Such examination might provide some framework on how to address black America's legitimate claim for restitution.

American slavery was grounded on a philosophy that was inherently racist. Only blacks could be slaves, yet blacks were not the only racial or ethnic groups encountered during the heyday of European "discoveries" of new places and the search for free labor and wealth. There were certainly other groups—Native American Indians, Hispanics, Asians, and many others. And there are historical accounts about the Spaniards and the Portuguese enslaving the indigenous populations. Yet there was something particularly attractive about black folks—their generosity and hospitality toward a stranger—that made it easier for them to become quick victims of the European appetite for economic exploitation and dislocation of Africa.

I agree with Randall Robinson that the black holocaust remains the most heinous human rights crime visited upon any group of people in the world over the past five hundred years. Certainly, as he says, other human rights crimes have resulted in the loss of millions of lives. But only slavery, Robinson argues passionately and rightly,

> with its sadistic patience, asphyxiated memory, and smothered cultures, has hulled empty a whole race of people with inter-generational efficiency. Every artifact of the victims' past cultures, every custom, every ritual, every god, every language, every trace element of a people's whole hereditary identity, wrenched from them and ground into a sharp, choking dust. It is a human rights crime without parallel in the modern world. For it produces its victims ad infinitum, long after the active stage of the crime has ended. Our children have no idea who they are. How can we tell them? How can we make them understand who they were before the ocean became a furnace incinerating every pedestal from which the ancient black muses had offered inspiration? What can we say to the black man on death row? The black mother alone, bitter, overburdened, and spent? Who tells them that their fate washed ashore at Jamestown with twenty slaves in 1619?[135]

Something must be done to change the terrible, negative feeling in black America that white American does not care. America is a better place when all of its citizens feel a part of it. If America is to move beyond race, then reparations for the crime of slavery are long overdue. Now is the time, not tomorrow.

Barack Obama and the Politics of Racial Classification

I'm not fully Korean and not fully white. I have an experience that puts me in the middle. And I want to recognize it.

Matt Kelley

The more mixed we are, the more likely it is that we will be sensitive to each other.

Beatriz Lopez-Flores

My personal feeling is that this is the beginning of the end of the overwhelming role of race in our public life.

Martha Farnsworth Riche

A blended America does not signal the beginning of the end of the role of race in our public life. For those who claim multiracial identities, they must also learn the cultural patterns and communication styles of the various groups that make up our society.

Ogom P. Nwosu

Barack Obama and the Politics of Racial Classification

Perhaps the most significant news from America's 2000 national profile on race and ethnicity is the portrait of an emerging group of Americans who now identify themselves as multiracial. In the nation's latest count of its population, the U. S. Census Bureau[136] reports that more than 6.8 million people described themselves as multiracial. This figure represents 2.4 percent of the nearly 289 million people who claim American citizenship. The projections are that by the year 2050, the number of Americans who will classify themselves as multiracial will reach 21 percent, a number that is almost a quarter of the country's current population. The impact is greatest in California, Arizona, Florida, New York, Texas, and New Mexico, states with large immigrant populations and tremendous diversity. The growing number of Americans who now identify themselves as multiracial in these regions can be explained by the increasing opportunities for interracial relationships. The opportunities brought about by immigration, for example, are fueling the possibilities for interracial friendships, interracial dating, and interracial marriages. The result is children with multiple identities, many of them unsure about how to classify themselves, and many of them choosing to identify themselves as multiracial.

It is also in this context that one must view the public reaction that visited Illinois Senator Barack Obama's announcement on February 10, 2007, regarding his candidacy to the office of the president of the U. S. Obama is the son of an African immigrant, Barack Hussein Obama, Sr. Like most African immigrants, his father came to study in the U. S., from the East African country of Kenya. "On the eve of Kenyan independence, he had been selected by Kenyan leaders and American sponsors to attend a university in the United States, joining the first large wave of Africans to be sent forth to master Western technology and bring it back to forge a new, modern Africa."[137] Young Obama's mother, Ann Dunham, a white native from Wichita, Kansas, met and married his father while both were enrolled at the University of Hawaii. After his parents divorced, the senior Obama went to Harvard University to pursue a doctorate degree. Obama's childhood years were spent in Hawaii and Indonesia. Even he has acknowledged the crisis of identity he experienced early on in his life resulting from this interracial marriage. In his 1995 book, Dreams from My Father, he writes about "my troubled heart, I suppose—the mixed blood, the divided soul, the ghostly image of the tragic mulatto trapped between two worlds." [138] In an interview on 60 Minutes[139] shortly after he announced his candidacy, the junior senator from Illinois was asked if he had "decided" to be black. "I am not sure I decided it," he responded. "If you look African American in this society, you're treated as African American. I am rooted in the African American community, but I am not defined by it." He then added: "I am comfortable in my racial identity, but that is not all I am."

Yet, even as he stakes a claim to his "blackness" in America, his candidacy has stirred up deep-seated feelings and questions in both black and white America about his identity and its implications for moving our nation beyond race. Reverend Al Sharpton's reaction, following Obama's announcement that "just because you are our color doesn't make you our kind," exposes entrenched perceptions in black America about black identity.[140] Melinda Chateauvert, assistant professor of African American Studies at the University of Maryland, explains that there is a perception in black America that "a personal connection to slavery and Jim Crow laws" remains "a common measure of who is and who isn't African American."[141] She also notes that what many do not recognize is the shift in the nature of black leadership from the leadership of the 1950s, which comprised church leaders, to a new generation of young people who may or may not have been exposed to slavery and Jim Crow laws. Obama represents this generation of young people. Thus his comment, "I am comfortable in my racial identity, but that is not all I am," is also instructive. The notion of "but that is not all I am" reflects some recognition of his other identity—his white identity and his experiences in Hawaii and Indonesia among Asians. In his latest book, The Audacity of Hope,[142] Obama writes, "I've never had the option of restricting my loyalties on the basis of race, or measuring my worth on the basis of tribe." He admits, in his words, to having "blood relatives who resemble Margaret Thatcher and others who could pass for Bernie Mac, so that family get-togethers over Christmas take on the appearance of a UN General Assembly meeting."[143] As Michael Fletcher notes in the Washington Post, "He identifies himself as African American, but his experiences are at once those of African Americans, whites, Asian Americans and immigrants."[144]

It is this recognition of his dual identity and multiple experiences that sets him apart from other black leaders and generates the excitement and support in white America and elsewhere (he is also one of us), and the possibilities for moving our nation beyond the politics of racial classification. In truth, given the history of the African American experience in this country, a significant number of African Americans can trace their roots to mixed or dual ancestries. Only recently did we learn publicly of the story of Essie Mae Washington-Williams, whom the family of the late Senator Strom Thurmond has now acknowledged is his illegitimate biracial daughter.

That we are at a place in our nation's history where people are willing to recognize and acknowledge all of their ancestral backgrounds suggests great promise for moving our nation beyond race. That public policy has been directed in that regard via our national head count is particularly significant because for the first time in America's census history, a person was allowed to recognize their multiracial identity on a government form. Certainly there are lessons and implications for cross-cultural understanding from this development. I will return to this point later in this chapter. But first I will discuss racial identity and our national head counts.

In the 1990 national count, Americans had five options to choose from regarding racial identity. In the 2000 national count, there were a whopping sixty-three options. Most Americans, according to the most recent polls, favor the multiplicity of options. For example, a USA Today/Gallup poll of 1,015 adults conducted in June 2001 showed nearly two-thirds of Americans (64 percent) in favor of the new classification. For these Americans, the multiracial classification is "good for the country," and many of them believe that Americans who come from dual or multiple racial identities ought "to think of themselves as multiracial rather than as belonging to a single race." [145] Of the adults interviewed in the USA Today/Gallup poll, 24 percent, however, viewed the new classification as bad for the country. Twelve percent had no opinion.

As the nation prepares for another count in 2010, we must examine the long-term implications of the new classification for moving our nation beyond race. First, where do we draw the line in the emerging politics of racial classification in America? In other words, will more groups call for their own categories, thus increasing the present sixty-three options? Second, will there be a day when race ceases to exist as a basis for social classification and national policies? Third, would Americans get along better if that happened? Put differently, would the prospects for effective human relations increase in a society where racial lines became more blurred? Would we become more sensitive towards each other as we became more mixed? Finally, would the new classification move our nation beyond race? These questions are critical in our continuing search for appropriate modalities for building a new vision of community in America.

The first question centers on where one draws the line on freedom to choose as different groups clamor for new classifications. Brazil is a classic example. The national census board, the Brazilian Institute of Geography and Statistics (IBGE), created 462 racial classification options. Everyone claimed that he or she was mixed with something, so that the experiment became too cumbersome, forcing the government to scrap the classification system. Like the U. S., Brazil conducts a national count every ten years, with the last one carried out in 2000. At the 2005 international conference of the Association for the Study of the Worldwide African Diaspora (ASWAD) held in Rio de Janeiro, Brazil, several Brazilian delegates with whom I spoke indicated that the scrapping of the classification system, on paper, may have signaled the death of race in Brazil's national life, but in practice, the nation has not moved beyond race. Brazil consists of several racial/ethnic groups including Europeans (mostly Portuguese, Germans, Italians, Poles), Africans, Hispanics, Asians (mostly Japanese, Chinese, Koreans), Arabs, and persons with distinct Indian origins. In their paper "From Ambiguity to Affirmation: Challenging Census Race Categories in Brazil,"[146] UCLA sociologists Stanley Bailey and Edward Telles provide a fascinating discussion about identity formation in Brazil since 1872, when the first national head count was conducted, to the changing racial dynamics in the country in recent years. Clearly, race remains central in Brazil's march toward building a more perfect nation and is present in every facet of national life. Race continues to matter in resource allocation, in income distribution, and in access to opportunities to advance one's place in society, issues that remain a huge problem for the national government.

Indeed, Brazil remains a nation polarized along racial lines according to the terms white, black, brown, and moreno, among others, and individuals continue to self-classify themselves beyond terms approved by the government. In such places as Rio de Janeiro, Saõ Paulo, and Salvador, Bahia, the challenge is more visible. Brazil's 1.5 million Japanese population is the largest Japanese population outside Japan, and its 70 million citizens of African descent represent the second largest concentration of black people in the world in one country after Nigeria, most of them living in the province of Bahia, in the country's Northeast region. If there are lessons to be learned from Brazil, it is that we must proceed with caution as we embark on the mission of broadening America's racial classification system.

Two former heads of the U. S. Census Bureau, Martha Farnsworth Riche and Kenneth Prewitt, have noted that the new racial classification system introduced by the Census Bureau does diminish the role of race in America's public life. In Farnsworth's words, the new classification signals "the beginning of the end of the overwhelming role of race in our public life."[147] And when race ceases to be meaningful, according to Kenneth Prewitt, "we're going to have to recreate ourselves as a society without using a set of social policies which are based on race."[148] I disagree. My position about moving our nation beyond race does not necessarily mean that race ceases to matter. Indeed if race as a classification system were to be scrapped completely, we would have to find other systems to carry out very important functions that national head counts typically perform: gathering critical demographic information that help us to address disparities, and gathering critical demographic information that help us understand emerging patterns in various aspects of public life, including health care and resource needs. These pieces of information are vital to crafting public policies and programs. Demographic data is also vital in advancing our understanding of various groups with respect to cultural patterns and communications styles. I will return to this point later.

True, new social distinctions along educational, geographical, and socio-economic lines, among others, may emerge to guide our calculations on social classifications and government policies. But without some effort to close the culture and attitude gaps, to tear down existing institutional structures which allow negative racial attitudes and feelings of superiority and inferiority to fester, without some effort to address long-standing historical inequities and inequalities in American society which have been shaped by race, the simple fact remains: no amount of classification or social distinction can diminish the role of race or move America beyond it. Those who suggest that the new multiracial classification signals the inevitability of the death of race in our national life need to rethink their position. If new census classifications (outside of race) are to become meaningful, they must be coupled with vigorous efforts to enforce anti-discrimination laws as they pertain to all areas of public and social life in America—employment, housing, lending, and entertainment. Already there are fears in black America that current "black-white divisions will be replaced by grievances between a tan America and a black America;"[149] In other words, fears that black-white divisions will be replaced with potential divisions between black America and other groups with different colors—a tan America. We see this already in the emerging frosty relations between Latinos and blacks.

A related question is whether the current classification will simply end at sixty-three options. Perhaps it will not. As we already know, millions of people who trace their ancestral roots to various regions of the world come to the U. S. As the groups expand and begin to gain more clout, they may be tempted to call for their own categories. Already, Arab Americans, who did not have a category of their own on the 2000 census form, have sent signals of their desire for such a category as the Census Bureau prepares for the next national count. At the moment, Arab Americans are classified as Caucasians, even though they do not see themselves as such. If the request is granted, certainly we will see a further increase in the current number of classifications. In a sense, we have opened a Pandora's box of agitation, uncertain of where this may lead America. We have begun, it seems to me, to create the foundation for a balkanized nation. And we have failed to couple this creation with any meaningful program for a new vision of community in America. This is a sad situation.

At issue also with the politics of racial classification is resource allocation. Many African Americans, for example, are concerned that the new classification may diminish their numerical superiority over other groups, and might cause them to lose money or access to expected resources. Increased numbers mean more dollars and more services are directed at particular communities and groups. Politicians who want votes pander to groups with high population counts. In doing so, they maximize their opportunities for election. We have seen this behavior in recent efforts to court various minority votes, especially the Hispanic votes, by different political parties. The proposal by the Bush administration to grant amnesty to several million illegal immigrants from Mexico ignores similar immigrants groups from other Latin American countries or other regions of the world. Implicit in the logic of this kind of politics is that there are more Hispanic immigrants to the U. S. who trace their origin to Mexico—a fact which clearly gives Mexico tremendous clout. But legal citizens of the U. S. who trace their origins to other countries in the Hispanic world are taking careful note. U. S. citizens who claim ancestral links to other regions of the world are also taking note. They too may have family members or friends who are illegal immigrants yet may be denied the benefits of a proposed amnesty because of a narrow-minded and shortsighted policy. In 1986, President Reagan granted amnesty to all illegal immigrants. There were no exceptions. It was an amnesty that did not criminalize anyone, but benefited everyone regardless of one's color, race, or national origin. It was the moral thing to do. I believe that amnesties like the one proposed by President Bush and Republican members of Congress are fundamentally flawed, potentially pitting those who benefit against those who do not. More importantly, they implicitly undermine both our ability to build an American community and any efforts to move our society beyond race.

Some have made the argument that the current approach to racial classification provides an opportunity for real choice; after all, our constitutional arrangement allows for a government of the people, by the people, for the people. Invariably, the democratization of choice in our approach to race and ethnicity as they pertain to the national count, which happens every ten years, provides one more way of demonstrating our type of constitutional order—the freedom to choose. But opening the door for more options in the classification system for our national profile on race and ethnicity requires the government to provide a stronger justification for denying those groups who may want to exercise the freedom to choose regarding their real heritage.

A Race-Neutral Society: Can We Get Along?

Amid the excitement, some have wondered whether Americans can get along better in a climate of an increasingly raceless, race-free, or race-neutral society. In other words, would the prospects for effective human relations increase where racial lines become more blurred? Would we become more sensitive toward each other? Martin Kasindorf and Haya El Nasser of USA Today provide a vivid picture of one perspective on this question: "Racial lines may blur until the melting pot idealized by playwright Israel Zangwill in 1908 becomes a harmonious, 'we-are-the-world' reality... The more mixed we are, the more likely it is that we will be sensitive to each other ... Who'll be left to hate?"[150]

Certainly this perspective on an increasingly race-neutral society suggests that individuals will develop a minimized consciousness about their racial background. This minimized consciousness about race may heighten one's identification with a potpourri of ethnic heritage. A person therefore claims multiple identities, which may lead to the formation of a third culture. If a third culture develops, a new system of behaving then emerges. The claim to multiple identities ultimately engenders, according to this perspective, sensitivity and empathy: "Who will be left to hate?" But this perspective is not necessarily supported by data or research in intercultural communication.

Problematic Vision

The vision of the blending of America, while rosy, is very problematic. First, the development of multiple identities, central to this vision, does not necessarily result in the rise of a third culture, nor does it lead to sensitivity or empathy. Second, it ignores the crucial role of culture in identity development as well as culture's role in human communication processes. We know from research that individuals with multiple identities are at least potentially linked to different ethnic groups through their parents and the other relationships they form. While some of these individuals may associate with their father's ethnic background, others may stress their identification with their mothers. In addition, certain structural forces in the society also inform the specific identities, chosen by individuals with multiple identities. These forces include the size of the ethnic group, the ethnic diversity in the region, and the perceptions these individuals hold regarding the nature of human communication among the different groups in the region. Physical characteristics also play some role in a person's choice of racial classification. In sum, therefore, identity formation and development emerge through a process of social interaction, and characterize the relationships that exist within a particular environment.[151]

Data from Chevelle Newsome's study of biracial children show that the choice about identities can be confirmed through racial enactment and communication, and that parents and other socialization agents can assist adolescents in their development of a racial identity by providing messages that are supportive and connote acceptance of the subject's choices.[152] Newsome's study sought to answer the following question: where do mixed-race children feel they belong in our world of European Americans, African Americans, Hispanic/Latino Americans, and Native Americans? Using a communication analysis approach, Newsome explored how mixed-race children frame and enact their racial identities, and how these identities are relationally and communally expressed, negotiated, and defined. The development of identity, she notes, is achieved through language, individual interaction with peers, and communication with parents/family. She concludes that biracial children tend to enjoy their dual ethnic identity and do not find it to be particularly burdensome to manage their competing ethnicities. Indeed her research provides further support for the new racial classification system adopted by the Census Bureau. Clearly the new system emerged in response to children who are compelled to choose one race when both parents come from dual or multiple racial backgrounds. The new system helps address this problem. However, the new classification system raises a more profound question about the children's cultural patterns and communication styles, and their ability to competently navigate an increasingly multicultural America. Which of the parent's cultural patterns and communication styles do they learn for this purpose?

Whose Cultural Backpacks?

The choice about racial classification shapes what culture a child learns. Thus, each individual, whether multicultural, bicultural, or monocultural, carries with him/herself a cultural backpack containing the cultural group's values, beliefs, attitudes, and norms. In this sense, a person's mindset shapes how the individual perceives others who are not members of his/her in-group, and how he or she relates to them. Certainly this perspective informs Reverend Sharpton's reaction to Senator Obama's membership in the African American community. In every society, therefore, individuals are part of the cultural base on which the meaning of behavior is premised. Molefi Asante calls this cultural base "the fundamental outlines of what we regard and preserve as characteristic of our society."[153] Yet most people in America just go about their business as if these fundamental outlines did not exist. Hall has noted how "most of culture lies hidden and is outside voluntary control, making up the warp and weft of human existence."[154] Since culture shapes the fundamental outlines of human existence, one must learn to become transcultural—that is, recognize what one's culture is and at the same time free oneself from that cultural prison, from the conventions and obsessions of that culture, and still at the same time expose oneself to the possibilities of other experiences.

To underscore this point, let me draw attention to a refreshing account from Molefi Asante regarding his encounter with the scholar and theologian Cornel West. I have come to admire both scholars. Asante writes, "In a videotaped debate with me, Cornel West said, 'Molefi Asante believes that one has to be centered, rooted, but I believe that one must go with the flow, move and groove, and be dynamic.' My reply was that I, too, believe that one must be 'open to the possibilities of dynamism, moving and flowing, but you have to be moving and flowing from some base. Those who do not move from a base are just floating in the air.'"[155]

As a student of intercultural communication, I am convinced that mere identification with multiple identities or a multiracial classification does not mean one is floating in the air. One may be raceless or race neutral, but not cultureless or culture-free. If we are to build a harmonious society and build a new vision of community in America, we must couple our new consciousness about multiracial identity with some knowledge of not only the culture we identify with, but also with a strong desire to learn about the cultural base for human behavior among other groups, and to put that knowledge into practice. Surely, a person's knowledge of other cultures is indispensable to effective human communication. If we are to move beyond race, we must proceed from a firm understanding that being multicultural does not mean one is cultureless. Thus while Senator Obama lays claim to a multiracial identity, he also stakes a claim to a culture that is deeply African American. "I am rooted in the African American community," he says. Each American, whether multicultural or multiracial, draws some strength from a certain cultural base. That is our history, and global societies also operate from similar foundations.

If we are to get along better as a nation, and as a people, we must proceed from the simple fact that classifying oneself as multicultural, bicultural, or monocultural does not mean one will be more sensitive towards others or that one has mastered the tools for communicating effectively with other people in a blended America or in a multicultural America. A blended America does not signal the beginning of the end of the role of race in our public life. For those who claim multiracial identities, they must also learn the cultural patterns and communication styles of the various groups that make up our society. In this way, we can move beyond race. This is the essential requirement for all Americans. This is the lesson from the story of Barack Obama. Now is the time to begin this process of intercultural growth.

❧ ⑩ ❧

Beyond 9/11: American Values and Global Influence

Indeed, it is precisely because of this nation's responsibilities and opportunities as a major power and as a symbol of ideals to which many of the world's people aspire that foreign languages, as a key to unlock the mysteries of other customs and cultures, can no longer be viewed as an educational or civic luxury.

Report of the President's Commission on Foreign
Languages and International Studies

There is no longer division between what is foreign and what is domestic—the world economy, the world environment, the world AIDS crisis, the world arms race—they affect us all.

President Bill Clinton

We act to defend ourselves and deliver our children from a future of fear. We choose the dignity of life over a culture of death. We choose lawful change and civil disagreement over coercion, subversion, and chaos. These commitments—hope and order, law and life—unite people across cultures and continents. Upon these commitments depend all peace and progress. For these commitments, we are determined to fight.

President George W. Bush

We stand for freedom and they hate it. We are rich and they envy us. We are strong and they resent it. All of which is true. But there are billions of poor and weak and oppressed people around the world. They don't turn planes into bombs. They don't blow themselves up to kill thousands of civilians. If envy were the cause of terrorism, Beverly Hills, Fifth Avenue and Mayfair would have become morgues long ago.

Fareed Zakaria

Beyond 9/11: American Values and Global Influence

What happened on that earth-shattering day of September 11, 2001 in the U. S., when nearly 3,000 people lost their lives, marked the beginning of a new kind of tactic in the resolution of international problems: the use of commercial airliners loaded with human beings to target significant institutions of our national life and to exact severe damage on our psyche. It seems to have succeeded.

We now live in a state of unending fear and suspicion. For the first time since World War II, we are witnessing a significant curtailment of basic freedoms and civil liberties in our country. We now live under a new Patriot Act that has given broad powers to the attorney general and the Department of Justice to arrest and detain citizens on a scale unrivalled before. The president has put in place a controversial new domestic surveillance program to monitor the domestic communications of American citizens as they engage in interactions with individuals abroad. We now know the National Security Agency, the nation's electronic watchdog, has been secretly collecting phone records of millions of American citizens on an unprecedented scale, with support provided by the telephone industry, in particular AT & T, BellSouth, and Verizon. We now have a new Department of Homeland Security, which has publicly emitted regular threat alert information that has altered our way of life.

Americans have become more cautious about traveling abroad. The airline industry nearly collapsed. Hotel and tourism businesses have faced hard times. Gasoline prices have soared. Unemployment numbers have gone up—the highest in some twenty years. Home foreclosures are now more numerous than during the Great Depression. Private sector investment is declining. Wall Street remains jittery.

We are seeing significant spending cuts on domestic priorities—in education and health care, programs that serve the poor. The cost of defending our freedom and our borders has placed additional strains on our budget. Nearly $400 billion of taxpayer's money has been spent on the war on terror so far, although paradoxically, an extraordinary tax cut, mostly for the wealthy, has been granted in a time of war. The result is a ballooning national debt standing at more than $8.4 trillion as of July 2006, the largest national debt since 1938. We are witnessing the emergence of a paranoid society, consumed by fear, and mistrustful of everyone, including ourselves.

The McCarthy era was similar, except the enemy was generally political rather than ethnic because we saw Russians as whites. Now the enemy is "ethnic" and our allies are whites, so more extreme legal and military measures are acceptable. We still accept the medieval belief that non-whites are not human unless we have Christianized them. U. S. Americans and Arabs (generally) no longer see Arabs/Muslims as white/Caucasian, as listed on the census forms of the past.

For a long while, we had assumed (except for some sporadic incidents, for example, the bombings of the World Trade Center in New York and the Federal Building in Oklahoma City) we were immune to incidents of terror, and that these events only took place in far flung places in the Middle East, Asia, and Africa. However, as the tragic events of 9/11 unfolded on television, it became clear that we have become, at least at home, a part of the equation of increasing global terror. We are now vulnerable at home, no longer as safe as we had thought. In the words of the African author Chinua Achebe (quoting Yeats and Eliot), things have fallen apart, and we are no longer at ease.

In the early hours of 9/11, my telephone rang at home. It was a call from my colleague and friend, Don Taylor at California State University, Sacramento. "I am sorry to wake you up," he began "but there is something going on in the country, and I'm not sure what it is. Planes are hitting buildings in New York. Turn on your TV quickly." For a brief moment, my heartbeat increased. It was clear from Taylor's voice that he was terrified. I jumped from my bed, quickly dashed to my television set to turn it on. Within seconds, I saw a plane crash into a tall structure. It was the second crash into the buildings that turned out to be the World Trade Center, the tallest buildings in the world, and the financial nerve center of our nation— the Twin Towers. I had instant flashbacks as I had visited those towers numerous times, the last time during a business trip in 1998. For the next several minutes, we watched and talked on the phone as the buildings and the people in them became engulfed in black smoke and a choking firestorm. There was massive confusion. Never before have I seen such destruction unfold live on television. Three thousand lives lost within minutes. Buildings razed to the ground. Assets worth billions of dollars wrecked. We could not stop it.

Firefighters, law enforcement officers, volunteers—all scurried to save some lives. America was helpless as metal rods and the steel on which the magnificent buildings stood melted to the ground. Elsewhere, in Washington, D. C., the nation's capital, the target was the Pentagon, the veritable symbol of American military might. It too was in smoke. We panicked. We wept. We mourned. And we vowed never again, never again.

While the target of 9/11 was our country and our people, what happened on that sad day also had a profound impact on the international community. Citizens of many faiths from more than eighty countries also lost their lives. On the morning of 9/11, I also received calls and emails from many friends and family members in Europe and Africa. They wanted to make sure that my family and I were fine. They wanted to know what they could do to help, and they wanted to learn more about what had happened. 9/11 brought the world closer to America, with enormous international sympathy for our loss and support for our course of action to locate and to punish the masterminds behind the cowardly attack on American soil. Indeed, forty-eight hours after the tragic events, the United Nations met in an emergency session to issue a strong condemnation. It was unanimous. An angry President Bush declared, "We are at war," as he went around the nation to soothe a wounded people.

We Face Enemies Who Hate Us?

In a sense, the war against terrorism has been an ongoing one, except that today it has become the centerpiece of American life and foreign policy. The breathtaking dimension of the terror of 9/11, reflected in the massive planning of the young men from the Middle East, the type of weapons used (our commercial airliners), and the magnitude of the casualties, has forced us to confront the new external challenges to our way of life. Since 9/11, we have witnessed repeated efforts to define and to explain away the tragic event as a struggle between good and evil, a struggle to protect our freedom, and to defend our values—because they hate us. In fact, as he addressed world leaders gathered in New York at the fifty-sixth General Assembly of the United Nations on November 10, 2001, an angry President Bush cast the struggle in these words: "As I've told the American people, freedom and fear are at war. We face enemies that hate not our policies, but our existence; the tolerance of openness and creative culture that defines us."[156] Many disagree.

Writing on *The Politics of Rage*, Newsweek editor Fareed Zakaria remarked, "We stand for freedom and they hate it. We are rich and they envy us. We are strong and they resent it. All of which is true. But there are billions of poor and weak and oppressed people around the world. They don't turn planes into bombs. They don't blow themselves up to kill thousands of civilians. If envy were the cause of terrorism, Beverly Hills, Fifth Avenue and Mayfair would have become morgues long ago."[157] Zakaria suggests that anger is certainly a natural and understandable reaction to the murder of thousands of innocent citizens of any country. "Yet anger," he says, "will not be enough to get us through what is sure to be a long struggle."[158] In a period of national emergency, it is tempting to look for easy explanations for what, after all, is a complicated problem. The president's explanations were too simplistic for a complicated problem whose genesis can also be traced to U. S. policies and communication style.

Policy and Communication

For all its pandemonium and horrific carnage, for all the justifiable anger and demand for revenge, what happened on September 11, 2001 was not necessarily because the enemies hate our existence, or envy our wealth, or resent our strength. We must be frank with ourselves. The attacks of 9/11 signified two things: first, a deep sense of cumulative hopelessness in the Arab and Islamic world with the policies of our government on fundamental regional issues, and second, our failure to communicate appropriately with the Arab and Islamic world on these crucial matters.

But the Arab and Islamic world are not alone. There is also a deep sense of frustration with U. S. policies in other regions, which reflect a lack of sensitivity to the cultural values and different communication styles of others. Those policies and insensitivities have made these regions vulnerable to international terrorism. In the past decade alone, for example, Kenya, Tanzania, and South Africa have become victims of such terror. Spain and the United Kingdom witnessed the worst terrorist attacks on their soil, resulting in the deaths of more than 250 people, 200 of them in Spain.

There is popular anger and resentment on the streets of Europe with the increasing American unilateral approach to international issues. Despite President Bush's assurances that the U. S. would consult with allies on missile defense, global warming, and international conflicts from the Balkans to Iraq, there is a perception in European capitals that the U. S. has proceeded alone on these matters, demonstrating a lack of will or ability to effectively communicate across cultural boundaries and an apparent lack of respect for others of different racial and cultural backgrounds.

Regarding the Kyoto Treaty to reduce global warming, we have been on the retreat. Bush's decision to scrap or fundamentally alter the 1972 Anti-Ballistic Missile Treaty, which prohibits building national missile defenses, as well as his opposition to creating an international criminal court, have been troubling to our allies. Regarding the Israeli-Palestinian conflict, we went on hiatus, only to resurface with a two-state road map. The road map unveiled in 2003 outlined a final and comprehensive settlement of the Israel-Palestine conflict by 2005. That has yet to happen. Indeed, the lack of progress on this front after much fanfare resulted in the emergence of the anti-American Hamas-led government, which the U. S. government has worked to undermine, in turn leading to a deterioration of the central government of the Palestinian people.

At the United Nations Human Rights Commission, we lost a seat we had held since 1947, when the commission was established. Washington had received written pledges of support from forty-one countries in the fifty-four-member commission. However, in the end, only twenty-nine delegates cast their votes for the U. S. in the secret balloting, won by France with fifty-two votes (Austria had forty-one and Sweden thirty-two).

The hostility against the U. S. has been growing even among traditional allies who view Washington's approach to international policies since the inception of the Bush administration as confrontational. The president's first term saw a new doctrine of pre-emptive strikes against suspected enemy nations, a departure from American foreign policy tradition, which made the international community restless. Even as we prepared to go to war against Iraq, we could not muster the needed support from the international community. And more than four years after Saddam Hussein was removed from power, there is no end in sight to America's presence in Iraq. Today, Iraq has become a misadventure of enormous proportions—over $200 billion spent, over 3,000 American lives lost, not counting the more than 50,000 Iraqis who have died, according to the president's estimates. How did it happen that a nation that had so much support after 9/11 squandered such international goodwill in less than a year?

How the Most Universal Nation Lost Goodwill

Three things have been central to America's influence around the world—our history, our values, and our people. In terms of its history and values, since wresting independence from England in 1776, America has sought to be a beacon of hope and freedom for people oppressed, and a shining example of representative government. We have stood on the side of liberty, prepared to defend it at every cost. The individual rights to create, to build, to worship, to bear arms if we so choose, and to live in dignity are the fundamental outlines of the just society that we seek. Every generation since the days of the founding fathers 230 years ago has worked to perfect our experiment, not for personal gain, but for public good. And through successive generations, we have seen the rewards of our hard work: freedom, opportunity, and a stronger, more prosperous society. In essence, as President Bush rightly remarked in his first address to the United Nations, America stands "for the permanent hopes of humanity."[159]

Because of our history and our values, the U. S. has become home to millions of people from many faiths and national origins in search of new life in the land of freedom and opportunity. We have become what some scholars have called the world's most truly universal nation, with every

144 Ogom P. Nwosu

corner of the globe represented in communities across our land. Many people who come to the U. S. do so because they cherish American values and the ideals of a universal nation. In this context, people around the globe expect that America's place as the most truly universal nation requires sensitivity, effective cross-cultural communication, and a more balanced and responsive approach to the formulation and implementation of international policies.

Saddam Hussein may have been a regional bully, but there is growing worry around the world that the U. S. is becoming the global bully. When we walk away from the ideals that make us a universal nation that stands for the permanent hopes of humanity, we lose the moral high ground.

Since World War II, we have played a vital role in managing and waging international peace and security. We led the efforts to rebuild Europe and Japan from the ashes of World War II and to create such international organs as the United Nations and its Security Council, the International Bank for Reconstruction and Development, the World Health Organization, and so on. Through the United Nations we made a commitment to resolving conflict through discourse, not coercion. For nearly fifty years after World War II, we waged a bitter and expensive Cold War with the Soviet Union, struggling for zones of influence across the globe in various continents in a bitter East-West rivalry in defense of our friends and our strategic interests. Throughout these years, we emerged more militarily powerful, and economically and culturally richer. By 1991, our policies with regard to the Soviet Union had worked. Without a single weapon fired at Moscow, the Soviet Union collapsed, leaving the U. S. as the world's only remaining superpower. Today, we have become what former secretary of state Madeleine Albright called the world's most indispensable nation, with the sole ability to project power around the world. The test of global leadership in a single-superpower world does not lie in our being feared, but rather in our being respected.

New Wine in an Old Bottle

Indeed the global angst and anger against the U. S. in recent years is not so much because it is the world's remaining superpower or the world's most indispensable nation. There, was after all, quiet jubilation in many foreign capitals that the bitter Cold War rivalry that had characterized international relations would at last come to a close. There was the sense, in Africa for instance, that global regions that were playgrounds for superpower competition and Cold War rivalry would receive a different kind of attention. There was a certain expectation around the world that multilateral approaches to serious international and regional issues would be sought. That has not been the case.

Anger against America rests essentially on the nature of our policies around the world, and how we have gone about pursuing those policies in a single-superpower world. In short, the global anger against the U. S. revolves around what many have called the arrogance of power. Steeped in the culture of the bitter Cold War rivalry of the past, like new wine in an old bottle, and intoxicated with the reality of being the world's most indispensable nation, U. S. policymakers, not quite prepared when the Soviet Union collapsed, and not quite clear how to proceed, were also not quite sure how to handle their new-found title and role as the sole remaining superpower.

Since the end of World War II, U. S. policy seemed clear and consistent, with a focus on the containment of Soviet communism and expansionism. In fact, during those Cold War years, there was a balance of both strength and terror on both sides of the East-West divide. This situation, many believe, secured international peace and security for nearly fifty years. At the end of the Cold War, and with the change in the international balance of power, policymakers were unsure how to proceed. The Bush Sr., Clinton, and Bush Jr. administrations have had different ideas about how to proceed and how to project American power and influence. The result has been a mélange of discordant voices and the collapse of continuity in policies that sent confusing messages about U. S. intentions in the new world order. The situation was not helped either by pronouncements from George W. Bush, when he came to office in 2001, young and inexperienced. The president's unilateral approach on virtually every international question and treaty has cost us more friends. The doctrine of pre-emption may well come to haunt us, as we have set the stage with our action in Iraq for other nations to take the laws into their hands, and to operate outside accepted international principles and legal norms. Given our actions, North Korea and Iran may well say goodbye to international principles and norms, i.e., the rule of law. No doubt, the misadventure in Iraq was a war of choice that has cost us respect and influence around the world.

Crisis of Communication in American Foreign Policy

The crisis in American foreign policy today in a single-superpower world may also lie in our inability to clearly define and communicate our goals and intentions, within the frameworks of international norms, and in a way that takes into account not just our strategic interests but also the sensitivities of other nations, in particular our allies. The resentment we have seen against our policies and our communication style or approach on these issues is not just in the Arab and Islamic world. Nigeria's Minister of State for Foreign Affairs, Dubem Onyia, in March 2003 described the nature of interaction between his government and Washington before the war in Iraq as amounting to "sheer intimidation."[160] Onyia, who had summoned the U.S. Ambassador to Nigeria Howard Jeter to his office to formally lodge his country's complaint, linked the suspension of U.S. military aid to Nigeria to his country's opposition to the invasion of Iraq. Similar sentiments came from Pretoria, where the South African government expressed concern with Washington's attempt to stop foreign leaders from making open comments contrary to U. S. position. And Chile complained about Washington's delay in signing a free-trade pact with it because of Santiago's soft support on the Iraqi question. We saw resentment in Europe among many of our allies, and among our friends in Asia, Latin America, and the Caribbean, not just among the leadership, but also among ordinary citizens. In December 2002, Pew Research Center released the findings of its Global Attitudes Project, which concluded that discontent against America "has grown around the world over the past few years. Images of the United States have been tarnished in all types of nations: among long-time NATO allies, in developing countries, in Eastern Europe and, most dramatically, in Muslim societies."[161] If we are to keep our friends and make new ones, we must cease our attribution of wrong motives to the behaviors and actions of virtually everyone who suggests alternatives.

The simplistic explanations of "old Europe" vs. "new Europe" offered by then-Secretary of Defense Donald Rumsfeld, and the comment from the president that "we face enemies that hate not our policies, but our existence," merely scratch the surface. Certainly, as the president remarked at the United Nations General Assembly on November 10, 2001, "no national aspiration, no remembered wrong can ever justify the deliberate murder of the innocent." In truth, as the president said, we must never tolerate "malicious lies that attempt to shift the blame away from the terrorists."[162] Clearly those who commit murderous acts must be pursued and brought to face justice, no matter how long it takes, but we must not permit the extremism in the behaviors of the bin Ladens to make us the new extremists and to cloud our judgment regarding how to best checkmate our increasing loss of influence around the world. We cannot always go it alone. Our trillion-dollar economy is inextricably tied to the global economy. We need friends to fight other battles.

We are at a critical crossroads in our nation's history and relations with the international community. "At a time when the resurgent forces of nationalism and of ethnic and linguistic consciousness so directly affect global relations, the U. S. requires far more reliable capabilities to communicate with its allies, analyze the behaviors of potential adversaries, and earn the trust and sympathies of the uncommitted. Yet, there is a widening gap between these needs and the American competence to understand and deal successfully in a world in flux."[163] Those conclusions made in 1979 by the President's Commission on Foreign Languages and International Studies remain very useful lessons for us today.

Our failure to resolve racial, ethnic, and cultural conflicts and inequalities at home impacts not just the life of our people and nation, but the lives of many peoples, and the peace and health of the world. We must strive to understand and communicate across racial, ethnic, and cultural boundaries; to hold many concepts of fairness, clusters of cultural values, cosmic schemas, and experiences of history simultaneously in our awareness;

to value others; to respect diversity; and to strive for a culture of civility. We must seek to act in a broadly just manner, not simply seek to control and punish the behavior of others who dare to disagree with us or be different from us. And we must act in concert with the rule of law, the very product we want to export abroad.

Notes

[1] "The O. J. Verdict," PBS Frontline. April 12, 2006.
http://www.pbs.org/wgbh/pages/frontline/oj/etc/script.html (accessed June 14, 2008).
[2] "Politicians speak out on Simpson verdict," CNN.com, October 3, 1995. http://www.cnn.com/US/OJ/verdict/political/index.html (accessed May 16, 2008).
[3] Randall Kennedy, "When Jurors Won't Convict Because of Race," *Sacramento Bee*, November 13, 1994. http://www.moderncourts.org/CJP/Reports/News/kennedy1.html (accessed May 17, 2008).
[4] Whitney Dow and Marco Williams, "Two Towns of Jasper," P.O.V. January 22, 2003. http://www.pbs.org/pov/pov2002/twotownsofjasper/aboutthefilm.html (accessed May 17, 2008).
[5] Ibid.
[6] "The Two Towns of Jasper. America in Black and White: Jasper, Texas with Ted Koppel." http://www.pbs.org/pov/pov2002/twotownsofjasper/about_townhall.html (accessed May 18, 2008).
[7] Pew Research Center, "Optimism about Black Progress Declines. Blacks See Growing Values Gap Between Poor and Middle Class," November 13, 2007, conducted in association with National Public Radio. http://pewsocialtrends.org/assets/pdf/Race.pdf (accessed May 17, 2008).
[8] Cindy Rodriguez, "Together, yet still apart. Attitudes soften, but blacks and whites see bias differently," *Detroit News*, July 19, 2007. http://www.detnews.com/apps/pbcs.dll/article?AID=/20070719/METRO/707190419/0/SPECIAL (accessed June 14, 2008).
[9] Ibid.
[10] James Carville, *We're Right, They're Wrong* (New York: Random House, 1999), 126–27.
[11] See Kimberly Neuendorf et al., "Explorations of the Simpson Trial 'Racial Divide,'" *Howard Journal of Communications* 11 (2000): 247–66.
[12] "O. J. Simpson. Race factor tilts the scales of public opinion," *USA Today*, February 2, 1997. http://www.usatoday.com/news/index/nns212.htm (accessed May 17, 2008).
[13] Ibid.
[14] Clarence Page, *Showing My Color: Impolite Essays on Race and Identity.* (New York: HarperCollins, 1996), http://www.washingtonpost.com/wp-srv/style/longterm/books/chap1/showingmycolor.htm (accessed May 20, 2008).
[15] See John Rawls, *A Theory of Justice* (Cambridge, MA: Harvard University Press, 1971); Robert Nozick, *Anarchy, State and Utopia* (New York: Basic Books, 1974); and Jennifer Hochschilds, *What's Fair: American Beliefs About Distributive Justice* (Cambridge, MA: Harvard University Press, 1981).
[16] "The State Bar of California: What Does It Do? How Does It Work?" http://www.calbar.ca.gov/calbar/pdfs/whowhat1.pdf (accessed May 17, 2008).
[17] Supreme Court of the United States. Opinion of the Court. No. 02-241. Barbara Grutter, Petitioner v. Lee Bollinger et al. On Writ of Certiorari to the United States Court of Appeals for the Sixth Circuit. Argued April 1, 2003-Decided June 23, 2003. October Term 2002. http://supreme.justia.com/us/539/306/ (accessed October 6, 2008).

[18] Ibid.

[19] Ibid, 14-15.

[20] U.S. Census Bureau. A Century of Change: America, 1900-1999. Public Information Office, December 20, 1999. http://www.census.gov/Press-Release/www/1999/cb99-ff17.html

[21] William Henry III, "Beyond the Melting Pot," *Time*, April 9, 1990. http://www.time.com/time/magazine/article/0,9171,969770,00.html (accessed October 5, 2008).

[22] "Republican Presidential Debate in New Hampshire," CNN.com, June 5, 2007. http://transcripts.cnn.com/TRANSCRIPTS/0706/05/se.01.html (accessed May 18, 2008).

[23] Ellis Cose, "The Rise of the New American Underclass. The real issue is not how many people to let in, but how to help them all fit in," *Newsweek*, December 22, 2007. http://www.newsweek.com/id/81598/output/print (accessed May 18, 2008).

[24] Ibid.

[25] Ali Mazrui, "Historical Struggles between Islamic and Christian Worldviews. An Interpretation," in *Transcultural Realities. Interdisciplinary Perspectives on Cross-Cultural relations,* ed. Virginia Milhouse, Molefi Asante, and Peter O. Nwosu (Thousand Oaks, CA: Sage Publications, 2001), 109.

[26] The term "affirmative effort" was first used as part of recommendations provided to a state agency following a comprehensive needs assessment by Nwosu & Associates. The consultants who worked on the project were myself, Dr. Don Taylor, and Dr. Virginia Kidd. Affirmative effort requires companies to make proactive efforts, in the absence of affirmative action laws, to diversify their workplaces.

[27] See for example Mary Ann Renz and John Greg, *Effective Small Group Communication* (Boston: Allyn & Bacon, 1999).

[28] American Leadership Forum. http://www.alfnational.org/ (accessed May 18, 2008).

[29] Roderick Paige, "Remarks on International Education in Schools" (paper presented at the meeting of the National Coalition on Asia and International Studies in Schools, Washington, D. C., November 20, 2002).

[30] Myron Lustig and Jolene Koester, *Intercultural Competence. Interpersonal Communication Across Cultures* (Boston: Allyn & Bacon, 2006), 25.

[31] Virginia Milhouse, Molefi Asante, and Peter Nwosu, "Introduction," in *Transcultural Realities*, ed. Milhouse, Asante, and Nwosu, ix.

[32] Ibid, x.

[33] Martin Luther King, Jr. (1963). Speech at Western Michigan University. Question and Answers. Archives and Regional History Collections, WMU. http://www.wmich.edu/library/archives/mlk/q-a.html (accessed October 6, 2008).

[34] Ibid

[35] Ron Stodghill and Amanda Bower, "Welcome to America's Most Diverse City," August 25, 2002. http://www.scribd.com/doc/219454/Welcome-to-Americas-Most-Diverse-City-TIME-3 (accessed May 18, 2008).

[36] Institute of International Education, "Open Doors Report: International Student Enrollment in U. S. Rose 6.4% in 2001–2002." http://www.iie.org/Template.cfm?Section=News_Announcements&template=/ContentManagement/ContentDisplay.cfm&ContentID=5470 (accessed May 21, 2008).

[37] Ibid.

[38] Center for Immigration Studies, "Immigrant Population at Record High in 2004." http://www.cis.org/articles/2004/back1204release.html (accessed June 14, 2008).

[39] Peter O. Nwosu, "Cultural Problems and Intercultural Growth. My American Journey," in *AmongUS. Essays on Identity*, 2nd ed., ed. Myron Lustig and Jolene Koester. (Boston: Allyn & Bacon, 2006), 84–92.

[40] The Igbo people of Nigeria are one of the largest ethnic groupings in Africa. Their population ranges from 15 to 25 million, according to various estimates. They occupy a land area (encompassing seven of Nigeria's thirty-one states—Abia, Anambra, Delta, Ebonyi, Enugu, Imo, and Rivers) that stretches from the south-eastern corner to the mid-western part of the country, and they also maintain considerable presence beyond their geographical region.

[41] Geert Hofstede, *Cultures and Organizations: Software of the Mind* (London: McGraw-Hill, 1991).

[42] The institution of warrant chief was introduced in Eastern Nigeria by the first British governor-general of Nigeria, Lord Frederick Lugard, as a system of indirect rule (i.e., governance through proxy) of subject territories.

[43] "Old boy" is an English (British) expression. There is an interesting irony here. America gained its independence from the English in 1776, yet the linguistic legacy from British rule has taken on different meanings over time in ways that impact forms of address in the two different societies.

[44] William Henry III, "Beyond the Melting P ot," *Time*, April 9, 1990, 28–31.

[45] Vision Circle: Electoral Politics, "Afro-Mex LA," July 12, 2005. http://cobb.typepad.com/visioncircle/electoral_politics/index.html (accessed June 14, 2008).

[46] Ibid.

[47] Edwin Aldarondo, "Hispanics Have Long and Rich History in United States," *New Bedford (CT) Standard-Times*, January 29, 2003, A13.

[48] Ibid.

[49] L. H. Gann and Peter J. Duignan, *The Hispanics in the United States. A History* (Boulder: Westview Press, 1986), xi.

[50] Ibid, xi.

[51] R. G. Castro, *Chicano Folklore: A Guide to the Folktales, Traditions, Rituals, and Religious Practices of Mexican-Americans* (New York: Oxford University Press, 2001): xiii.

[52] Gann and Duignan, *The Hispanics in the United States*, 16.

[53] U. S. Census Bureau, "Coming to America: A Profile of the Nation's Foreign-Born," January 2002. http://www.census.gov/prod/2002pubs/cenbr01-2.pdf (accessed June 14, 2008).

[54] Jeffrey Passel and D'Vera Cohn, Pew Research Center, "Immigration to Play Lead Role In Future U. S. Growth. U. S. Population Projections: 2005–2050," February 11, 2008. http://pewresearch.org/pubs/729/united-states-population-projections (accessed June 14, 2008).

[55] Richard Rodriguez, *Hunger of Memory: The Education of Richard Rodriguez* (Toronto: Bantam Books, 1982), 15–16.

[56] Nicolas C. Vaca, *The Presumed Alliance. The Unspoken Conflict between Latinos and Blacks and What It Means for America* (New York: HarperCollins, 2004), 105.

[57] Julianne Malveaux, "Black and Brown People: Coalition or Competition?" *Black Issues in Higher Education* 15, no. 20 (1998): 42.

[58] Ibid.

[59] Comment made in personal conversation with Peter O. Nwosu on March 10, 2003, Sacramento, California.

[60] Martin Luther King, Jr., *A Testament of Hope. The Essential Writings and Speeches of Martin Luther King, Jr.* (San Francisco: Harper & Row, 1986), 17.

[61] Martin Luther King, Jr., "Letter from a Birmingham Jail," April 16, 1963. http://www.africa.upenn.edu/Articles_Gen/Letter_Birmingham.html (accessed June 18, 2008).

[62] Martin Luther King, Jr., *Strength to Love* (New York: Harper & Row, 1963), 36.

[63] Daniel Macalllair. America's One-Million Nonviolent Prisoners. (2002). http://www.cjcj.org/pubs/one_million/onemillion.html#32

[64] Stephen Hartnett, "Prison Labor and Capitalism in Historical Perspective." (c.1997). http://www.historyisaweapon.com/defcon1/hisprislacap.html (accessed June 15, 2008).

[65] Mike Davis, "Hell Factories in the Field: A Prison-Industrial Complex," February 20, 1995. http://www.radicalurbantheory.com/mdavis/hellfactories.html (accessed June 15, 2008).

[66] California Department of Corrections and Rehabilitations. http://www.cdcr.ca.gov/Career_Opportunities/POR/Pay.html (accessed November 16, 2007).

[67] The California State University, http://csucareers.calstate.edu/careers/search.asp?PositionType=1; and Wyatt Hume and Clifford Brunk, "Faculty Appointment and Advancement: Building and Sustaining a Preeminent Faculty at the University of California," November 17, 2005. http://www.universityofcalifornia.edu/regents/regmeet/nov05/302pp.pdf (accessed November 16, 2007).

[68] "Three Strikes Law Disproportionately Affects Blacks," *Sacramento Observer*, October 27, 2004. http://www.afro-netizen.com/2004/10/three_strikes_1_1.html (accessed June 22, 2008).

[69] California Department of Corrections and Rehabilitation, "Average Daily Prison Population. Calender Year 2006," January 2007. http://www.cdcr.ca.gov/Reports_Research/Offender_Information_Services_Branch/Annual/IPOP2/IPOP2d0612.pdf (accessed November 16, 2007).

[70] California Department of Corrections and Rehabilitation, "Fourth Quarter 2007, Facts and Figures." http://www.cdcr.ca.gov/Divisions_Boards/Adult_Operations/Facts_and_Figures.html (accessed November 16, 2007).

[71] U. S. Census Bureau, "California: 2006 American Community Survey Data Profile Highlights." http://factfinder.census.gov/servlet/ACSSAFFFacts?_event=&geo_id=04000US06&_geoContext=01000US%7C04000US06&_street=&_county=&_cityTown=&_state=04000US06&_zip=&_lang=en&_sse=on&ActiveGeoDiv=geoSelect&_useEV=&pctxt=fph&pgsl=040&_submenuId=factsheet_1&ds_name=null&_ci_nbr=&qr_name=&reg=%3A&_keyword=&_industry= (accessed November 16, 2007).

[72] Hispanics/Latinos who consider themselves white, black, or other are counted twice in the U. S. Census Bureau data.

[73] California Department of Corrections and Rehabilitation, "Summary Fact Sheet," January 2007. http://www.cdcr.ca.gov/Reports_Research/summarys.html (accessed November 16, 2007).

[74] "Child Population, by Race and Ethnicity: 2007," Kidsdata.org. http://www.kidsdata.org/topictables.jsp?csid=0&t=24&i=7&ra=3_132 (accessed November 16, 2007).

[75] Dorothy Roberts, *Shattered Bonds. The Color of Child Welfare* (New York: Basics, 2002), 8.

[76] Dr. Toni Humber. California State Polytechnic University, Pomona. Personal conversation. June 12, 2007.

[77] John Mercurio. Lott apologizes for Thurmond comment. Gore lasts statement as 'racist'. Tuesday, December 10, 2002. http://archives.cnn.com/2002/ALLPOLITICS/12/09/lott.comment/ (accessed September 5, 2008).

[78] Winthrop D. Jordan, *White over Black. American Attitudes toward the Negro 1550–1812* (Baltimore: Penguin Books, 1968).

[79] Cornel West, *Race Matters* (New York: Vintage, 1994), x.

[80] Erica Goode, "With Video Games, Researchers Link Guns to Stereotypes," *New York Times*, December 10, 2002. http://query.nytimes.com/gst/fullpage.html?res=9A00E5DE163AF933A25751C1A9649C8B63 (accessed June 16, 2008).

[81] "Race and Income: Exploring Racial Differences in Income," About.com: Race Relations. http://racerelations.about.com/od/raceandwork/a/raceandincome.htm (accessed June 16, 2008).

[82] Ibid.

[83] Clifton Castell, "Teacher-Student Interactions and Race in Integrated Classrooms," *Journal of Educational Research* 92, no. 2 (1998): 111.

[84] "True Colors," *Primetime*, ABC News, VHS, 19 minutes, 1991. In this *Primetime* episode, correspondent Diane Sawyer and a video documentary crew follow two men (one white and one black) through the day in St. Louis, Missouri.

[85] Ibid.

[86] Stephen Labaton, "The Media Business: Advertising; The Government's First Study on Discrimination in Radio Advertising Finds a Lot of Fodder," *New York Times*, January 14, 1999. http://query.nytimes.com/gst/fullpage.html?res=9B04EED81231F937A25752C0A9 6F958260&sec=&spon=&pagewanted=all (accessed June 22, 2008).

[87] Institute of Medicine, *Unequal Treatment: Confronting Racial and Ethnic Disparities in Health Care* (Washington, D. C.: The National Academic Press, 2003).

[88] Bill Dedman, The Color of Money: Blacks turned down for home loans from S&Ls twice as often as whites. The Atlanta Journal Constitution, January 22, 1989, A1. http://PowerReporting.com/color/53.html.

[89] Helen F. Ladd, "Evidence on Discrimination in Mortgage Lending," *Journal of Economic Perspectives* 12, no. 2 (1998): 46–62.

[90] Benny Kass, "Minority Home Owners Hit Hard by Predatory Lenders." http://realtytimes. com/rtpages/20011119_predatory.htm (accessed June 17, 2008).

[91] "Study: Housing Discrimination Makes Case for Reparations for Black Americans," Oregon State University, January 14, 2008. http://oregonstate.edu/dept/ncs/newsarch/ 2008/Jan08/reparations.html (accessed June 17, 2008).

[92] Ibid.

[93] Roberts, *Shattered Bonds*, 74.

[94] A. Hines, J. Merdinger, P. Lee, and M. Coach, M., "An Evaluation of Factors Related to the Disproportionate Representation of Children of Color in Santa Clara County's Child Welfare System. Exploratory Phase" (a report of the Child Welfare Research Team, San Jose State University, San Jose, California, 2001).

[95] Roberts, *Shattered Bonds*, 17.

[96] Personal communication with Gil Villagran, Child welfare advocate, (2003).

[97] Roberts, *Shattered Bonds*, 55.

[98] Ann Garland, Elissa Ellis-MacLeod, John A. Landsverk, William Ganger, and Ivory Johnson, "Minority Populations in the Child Welfare System. The Visibility Hypothesis Reexamined," *American Journal of Orthopsychiatry* 68 (1998): 142–43.

[99] CWS Stakeholders' Group. "Building a Culture of Fairness and Equity in California's Child Welfare System." In <u>CWS Stakeholders Group CWS Redesign: Conceptual Framework, May 2002</u>, p158. Sacramento, California: Report of the California Department of Social Services.

[100] Superior Court of California, Sacramento County Juvenile Justice Initiative, "Report of the Task Force on Fairness" (Sacramento, CA, August 1994).

[101] Superior Court of California, County of Sacramento. "Exploring the Factors to Disproportionate Minority Confinement (DMC) in the Sacramento County Juvenile Justice System" (report of the Sacramento County Disproportionate Minority Confinement Research Committee submitted to the Sacramento Criminal Justice Cabinet, July 1999), 11.

[102] Amnesty International, "Betraying the Young: Human Rights Violations Against Children in the US Justice System," November 20, 1998. http://asiapacific.amnesty.org/library/ Index/ENGAMR510571998?open&of=ENG-392 (accessed June 17, 2008).

[103] Sacramento County DMC Research Committee, "Exploring," 13.

[104] Human Rights Watch, "Punishment and Prejudice: Racial Disparities in the War on Drugs," *Alcoholism & Drug Abuse Weekly* 12, no. 25 (2000): 7.

[105] "Media Portrays Most Poor People as Black—Yale University Study," *Jet*, September 8, 1997. http://findarticles.com/p/articles/mi_m1355/is_n16_v92/ai_19767372 (accessed June 17, 2008).

[106] See W.E.B. Du Bois, *The Souls of Black Folk* (Boston: Dutton, 1903).

[107] "Transcript of Bush's Address to N.A.A.C.P.," *The New York Times*, July 20, 2006. http://www.nytimes.com/2006/07/20/washington/20text-bush.html?pagewanted=3 (accessed June 16, 2008).

[108] West, *Race Matters*, 63–64.

[109] Carville, *We're Right, They're Wrong*, 129.

[110] David Horowitz, "Ten Reasons Why Reparations for Slavery Is a Bad Idea. And Racist Too," FrontPageMagazine.com, January 03, 2001. http://www.frontpagemag.com/Articles/Read.aspx?GUID=23D875B0-65A3-44A3-A27B-14831CCB4107 (accessed June 6, 2008).

[111] Ibid.

[112] Howard Zinn, *A People's History of the United States* (New York: Harper & Row, 1980), 28.

[113] Chancellor Williams, *The Destruction of Black Civilization. Great Issues of a Race from 4500 B. C. to 2000 A. D.* (Chicago: Third World Press, 1987), 23.

[114] Zinn, *People's History*, 28.

[115] Randal Robinson, *The Debt. What America Owes to Blacks* (New York: Dutton Books, 2000), 33.

[116] Zinn, *People's History*, 29.

[117] Martin Luther King, Jr., *Where Do We Go From Here. Chaos or Community?* (Boston: Beacon Press, 1967), 75.

[118] "Remarks by President Bush...," July 8, 2003. http://www.whitehouse.gov/news/releases/2003/07/20030708-1.html (accessed June 6, 2008).

[119] James Bennett, "Clinton in Africa: Overview; In Uganda, Clinton Expresses Regret on Slavery in U. S.," *New York Times*, March 25, 1998. http://query.nytimes.com/gst/fullpage.html?res=9B04E7DF1E38F936A15750C0A96E958260 (accessed June 6, 2008).

[120] Myron Lustig and Jolene Koester, *Intercultural Competence. Interpersonal Communication Across Cultures* (Boston: Allyn & Bacon, 2006), 156.

[121] Phyllis A. Katz and Dalmas Taylor, "Introduction," in *Eliminating Racism: Profiles in Controversy*, ed. Phyllis A. Katz and Dalmas A. Taylor (New York: Plenum, 1988).

[122] Peggy McIntosh, "White Privilege: Unpacking the Invisible Knapsack." http://seamonkey.ed.asu.edu/~mcisaac/emc598ge/Unpacking.html (accessed June 6, 2008).

[123] Project Hip-Hop, 1997, quoted in Ella Mazel, *"And don't call me a racist!"* (Lexington, MA: Argonaut Press, 1998), 13.

[124] McIntosh, ibid.

[125] McIntosh, ibid.

[126] McIntosh, ibid.

[127] Robinson, *The Debt*, 9.

[128] Chorzow Factory case, Germany v. Poland, 1928, cited in Lloyd Stewart, *A Far Cry from Freedom: Gradual Abolition, 1799–1827* (Bloomington, IN, AuthorHouse, 2005), 360.

[129] Lord Anthony Gifford, "The Legal Basis of the Claim for Reparations" (paper presented at the First Pan-African Congress on Reparations, Abuja, Nigeria. April 27–29, 1993).

[130] Chinweizu, "Reparations and a New Global Order: A comparative overview" (paper presented at the First Pan-African Congress on Reparations, Abuja, Nigeria. April 27–29, 1993).

[131] "Report Reveals Blacks Now Outnumber Whites on U. S. Welfare Rolls," *Jet*, August 17, 1998. http://findarticles.com/p/articles/mi_m1355/is_n12_v94/ai_21020055 (accessed June 22, 2008).

[132] King, Jr., *Where Do We Go from Here*, 105.

[133] King, Jr., *Where Do We Go from Here*, 105–6.

[134] Ali Mazrui, "A Leading Voice," *Africanwatch: The Authentic Voice* 1, no. 1 (1999): 24–5.

[135] Robinson, *The Debt*, 216–17.

[136] Sharon Lee, "A Kids Count/PRB Report on Census 2000. Using the New Racial Categories in the 2000 Census," a project of the Annie E. Casey Foundation and the Population Reference Bureau, March 2001. http://www.prb.org/pdf/census2000_usingnewracialprofiles.pdf (accessed June 6, 2008).

[137] Barack Obama, *Dreams from My Father* (New York: Three Rivers Press, 1995), 9.

[138] Obama, *Dreams*, xv.

[139] Steve Kroft, "Transcript Excerpt of Interview with Senator Barack Obama," *60 Minutes*, February 11, 2007. http://www.cbsnews.com/stories/2007/02/11/60minutes/main2458530.shtml (accessed June 6, 2008).

[140] Leslie Fulbright, "Obama's Candidacy Sparks Debates on Race. Is He African American if his Roots Don't Include Slavery?" *San Francisco Chronicle*, February 19, 2007. http://www.sfgate.com/cgi-bin/article.cgi?f=/c/a/2007/02/19/MNG3AO7BT41.DTL (accessed June 6, 2008).

[141] Ibid.

[142] Barack Obama, *The Audacity of Hope. Thoughts on Reclaiming the American Dream* (New York: Crown Publishers), 231.

[143] Ibid, 231.

[144] Michael Fletcher, "Obama's Appeal to Blacks Remains an Open Question," *Washington Post*, January 25, 2007. http://www.washingtonpost.com/wpdyn/content/article/2007/01/24/AR2007012402032.html (accessed June 6, 2008).

[145] Martin Kasindorf and Haya El Nasser, "Impact of Census' Race Data Debated." *USA Today*, March 12, 2001. http://www.usatoday.com/news/nation/census/2001-03-12-censusimpact.htm (accessed June 6, 2008).

[146] Stanley R. Bailey and Edward E. Telles, (2002). "From Ambiguity to Affirmation: Challenging Census Race Categories in Brazil." http://www.sscnet.ucla.edu/soc/faculty/telles/Paper_AffirmationandAmbiguity.pdf (accessed June 6, 2008).

[147] Kasindorf and El Nasser, ibid.

[148] Kasindorf and El Nasser, ibid.

[149] Kasindorf and El Nasser, ibid.

[150] Kasindorf and El Nasser, ibid.

[151] Michael Hecht, Mary J. Collier, and Sidney Ribeau, *African American Communication: Ethnic Identity and Cultural Interpretation* (Newbury Park, CA: Sage, 1993).

[152] Chevelle Newsome, "Multiple Identities. The Case of Biracial Children," in *Transcultural Realities. Interdisciplinary Perspectives on Cross-Cultural Relations*, ed. Virginia Milhouse, Molefi Asante, and Peter Nwosu (Newbury Park, CA: Sage, 2001).

[153] Molefi Asante, "Transcultural Realities and Different Ways of Knowing," in *Transcultural Realities. Interdisciplinary Perspectives on Cross-Cultural Relations,* ed. Virginia Milhouse, Molefi Asante, and Peter O. Nwosu (Newbury Park, CA: Sage, 2001), 77.

[154] Edward Hall, *The Hidden Dimension* (New York: Anchor Books, 1969), 188.

[155] Asante, "Transcultural Realities," 77.

[156] George W. Bush, "First Address to the General Assembly of the United Nations in New York City," November 10, 2001. http://www.september11news.com/PresidentBushUN.htm (accessed May 26, 2008).

[157] Fareed Zakaria, "The Politics of Rage: Why Do They Hate Us?" Newsweek, October 15, 2001. http://fareedzakaria.com/ARTICLES/newsweek/101501_why.html (accessed October 4, 2008).

[158] Ibid.

[159] Bush, ibid.

[160] Adeyeye Joseph, "U.S.-Nigeria Relations: On a Dangerous Bend," *THISDAY Online.* http://www.thisdayonline.com/archive/2003/03/29/20030329cov01.html (accessed May 26, 2008).

[161] Pew Research Center, "What the World Thinks in 2002. How Global Publics View: Their Lives, Their Countries, The World, America." http://people-press.org/reports/display.php3?ReportID=165 (accessed June 6, 2008).

[162] Bush, ibid.

[163] "Strength Through Wisdom: A Critique of U.S. Capability" (a report to the president from the President's Commission on Foreign Languages and International Studies, Washington, D. C. Department of Health, Education, and Welfare, 1979), 1–2.

Bibliography

Amnesty International "Betraying the Young: Human Rights Violations Against Children in the US Justice System." November 20, 1998. http://asiapacific.amnesty.org/library/Index/ENGAMR510571998?open&of=ENG-392.

Carville, James. *We're Right, They're Wrong*. New York: Random House, 1996.

Cose, Ellis. "The Rise of the New American Underclass." *Newsweek*, December 22, 2007. http://www.newsweek.com/id/81598/output/print.

Dow, Whitney, and Marco Williams. "Two Towns of Jasper." *P. O. V.*, January 22, 2003. http://www.pbs.org/pov/pov2002/twotownsofjasper/aboutthefilm.html.

Du Bois, W. E. B. *The Souls of Black Folk*. Boston: Dutton, 1903.

Gann, L. H., and P. J. Duignan. *The Hispanics in the United States. A History*. Boulder, CO: Westview Press, 1986.

Hecht, Michael J., Sidney A. Ribeault, and Mary Jane Collier. *African American Communication: Ethnic Identity and Cultural Interpretation*. Newbury Park, CA: Sage Publications, 1993.

Henry, William III. "Beyond the Melting Pot." *Time*, April 9, 1990. http://www.time.com/time/magazine/article/0,9171,969770,00.html.

Jordan, Winthrop. *White over Black. American Attitudes toward the Negro: 1550–1812*. Baltimore: Penguin, 1968.

Katz, Phyllis A., and Dalmas A. Taylor, eds. *Eliminating Racism: Profiles in Controversy*. New York: Plenum, 1988.

King, Martin Luther, Jr. *A Testament of Hope. The Essential Writings and Speeches of Martin Luther King, Jr.* Edited by James M. Washington. San Francisco: Harper & Row, 1986.

Lustig, Myron, and Jolene Koester, eds. *AmongUS. Essays on Identity*. 2nd ed. Boston: Allyn & Bacon, 2006.

Malveaux, Julianne. (1998). "Black and Brown People: Coalition or Competition?" *Black Issues in Higher Education*. 15, no. 20 (1998). http://findarticles.com/p/articles/mi_m0DXK/is_/ai_53459619.

McIntosh, Peggy. "White Privilege: Unpacking the Invisible Knapsack." 2001. http://seamonkey.ed.asu.edu/~mcisaac/emc598ge/Unpacking.html.

Milhouse, Virginia, Molefi Asante, and Peter Nwosu, eds. *Transcultural Realities. Interdisciplinary Perspectives on Cross-Cultural Relations*. Newbury Park, CA: Sage Publications, 2001.

Page, Clarence. *Showing My Color. Impolite Essays on Race and Identity*. New York: HarperCollins, 1996.

Roberts, Dorothy. *Shattered Bonds. The Color of Child Welfare*. New York: Basic Civitas Books, 2002.

Index

About the Author:

Ogom P. Nwosu graduated from Howard University, where he served as president of the Graduate Student Council in the John H. Johnson School of Communications. He is American Council on Education (ACE) Fellow, Office of the President at Tennessee State University, Nashville, and special assistant on diversity initiatives to the provost and vice president for academic affairs at California State University, Northridge. Prior to these assignments, Professor Nwosu was chair, departments of communication studies, and urban studies and planning at Northridge. A nationally recognized expert on communication and diversity, his work includes consultation and technical support to public and private agencies on strategies for incorporating fairness and equity in planned programs of change. A former Fulbright scholar in South Africa, he is author of several scholarly works, including two books: *Transcultural Realities: Interdisciplinary Perspectives on Cross-Cultural Relations and Communication* and the *Transformation of Society: A Developing Region's Experience.*